Bloom

a Girl's Guide To Growing Up

with Brio Magazine's Susie Shellenberger

Bloom

a Girl's Guide To Growing Up

with Brio Magazine's Susie Shellenberger

FOCUS ON THE FAMILY

TYNDALE

Bloom
a Girl's Guide To Growing Up
with Brio Magazine's Susie Shellenberger

Library of Congress Cataloging-in-Publication Data
Bloom : a girl's guide to growing up.— 1st ed.
p. cm.
Summary: Practical advice from a Christian viewpoint about the internal
and external changes experienced by teenage girls, touching on
everything from shopping wisely to good hygiene to eating disorders.
ISBN 1-58997-061-6
1. Girls—Religious life—Juvenile literature. 2. Girls—Conduct of
life—Juvenile literature. [1. Puberty. 2. Teenage girls. 3. Christian life.]
I. Tyndale House Publishers.
BV4551.3 .B58 2003
248.8'33—dc21

                                                    2003007988

Focus on the Family books are available at special quantity discounts when
purchased in bulk by corporations, organizations, churches, or groups.
Special imprints, messages, and excerpts can be produced to meet your needs.
For more information, contact: Resource Sales Group, Focus on the Family, 8605 Explorer Drive,
Colorado Springs, CO 80920; or phone (800) 932-9123.

Editors: Kathy Davis and Mick Silva
Design: Lance Blanchard and Rob Brinton

Printed in Singapore
2 3 4 5 6 7 8 9 / 09 08 07 06 05 04

Meet the Contributors

Susie Shellenberger

Susie is the founding editor of *Brio* magazine and *Brio & Beyond*. She's a former high school teacher and youth pastor who's ridden camels in India, elephants in Thailand, safaried in Africa, and has been to every continent in the world—yep, even Antarctica! Susie is a national youth speaker and has written 30 books. She's also a Coca-Cola nut and even has a 1950s machine in her basement so there's never a shortage of her fave soft drink.

Kathy Gowler

Kathy is the editorial assistant and missions coordinator for *Brio* magazine. She loves traveling and ministering to teens and has been to all seven continents too! Her fave is Africa! She and her husband, Jeff, have been married 25 years, and she is the proud mom of Matthew and Kelly, and mom-in-law to Tiffany.

Andrea Stephens

When not playing with her golden retrievers, working on a painting, or munching pepperoni pizza with extra cheese, Andrea is writing (she is up to 12 books so far) or answering questions in *Brio* magazine. Of course, she might be presenting a BABE Seminar or studying for a college exam. No matter what she's doing, you can be sure she loves teen girls! Andrea lives in Bakersfield, California with her handsome pastor—who is also her husband!

Marty Kasza

Marty is the associate editor of *Brio* magazine and lives in Colorado Springs, Colorado. When she is not hiking to the bottom of the Grand Canyon for a *Brio* story, creating the *Brio* Web site, or having a blast working on the magazine, Marty loves to spend time with her husband, Brent. You'll find the two of them making improvements on their home or taking weekend trips to the mountains.

Jodi Carlson

Jodi lives in Bend, Oregon, where she hikes mountain trails by summer and cozies up on her couch by winter. She enjoys conversations with dear friends, exciting social scenes, studying psychology and philosophy, and eating ice cream.

Bob Smithouser

Bob is an entertainment expert, editor of *Plugged In* magazine, and general editor of *Movie Nights*. Bob also writes High Voltage, a popular column in Brio.

Richard Bergland

Richard was an elementary P.E. teacher in Bryan, Texas, for seven years. After that, he taught high school English and coached football and baseball for 16 years. He has been married to his wife, Jennifer, for 24 years and they have three children, Mallory, 17, David, 14, and Stephanie, 10. He is a youth worker, and is on the drama team of Bryan Church of the Nazarene. His hobbies include golf, fishing, working out, and being outdoors.

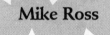

Mike Ross

Mike is the editor of *Breakaway* a national magazine for teen guys published by Focus on the Family. Communicating with teenagers is his passion. Mike has written a bunch of books for young people.

Jeremy V. Jones

Jeremy is the associate editor of *Breakaway.* His job takes him all over the country, landing interviews with athletes, musicians, and cool, everyday teens just like you. Highlights include learning to shred for a surfing story and hanging out with some firefighters for a write-up on these brave men and women.

Chuck Johnson

Chuck is the director of periodicals at Focus on the Family. In other words, he spends his time leading and motivating people. (Hey, he used to be a high school principal, so he has lots of experience!)

Jeff Edmondson

Jeff is a cool youth guy (he speaks to teens all over the world), a contributor to *Breakaway,* and a card-carrying sci-fi fan. He's practically a walking Star Trek encyclopedia!

Contents

Introduction

Part One:
Being Woman

Part Two:
Dating & Relating

Introduction

One of the most loved and hated attractions at any amusement park is probably the Fun House—that maze of weird mirrors and hallways that never seem to end. It's a challenge to find your way through the maze. And along the way, you see yourself in mirrors that make you look tall and skinny, or short and fat.

But the Fun House can also be frustrating when the maze gets a little too challenging. And after a while, it becomes less fun to see yourself in the other mirrors—the ones that play dirty tricks on your reflection.

Those Fun Houses are a lot like growing up. It's a fun challenge to discover your personality, the secret of making and keeping friends, and the wonderful feeling of becoming a woman. But handling zits, rejection, and a changing body full of hormones can get frustrating really fast!

That's why we wrote this book. We want to help these years of discovery be more fun and less frustrating. We've tried to include the most important things you'll need to know to make it through the maze, so that when you hit a dead-end, you'll be able to simply pick up this book and find the chapter that speaks to where you're at.

And if you ever get to a place that feels scary or all alone, just close your eyes and imagine this book as a great big hug. Most of all, that's what we wanted to do in this book—to let you know that we understand, we're here for you, and we're hugging you right through the pages. We hope you can feel that.

Susie Shellenberger

Editor, *Brio* Magazine
brio@macmail.fotf.org

(If you'd like to receive a sample copy of *Brio* magazine for girls ages 12 to 15 or *Brio & Beyond* for girls 16 and older, just drop us a note. We'd love to hear from you.)

Part One
Being Woman

Am I Normal?

One word best describes your life right now: CHANGE! Your body is literally a chemical laboratory that's exploding with all kinds of new activity. And with all these changes going on inside (and outside), you can't help asking yourself, *Is this normal? Am I normal?*

Maybe every other girl has gotten her period except you. Or maybe your best friend is a size C and you're still in the Triple A Club. Some girls already begin to look womanly in middle school . . . complete with breasts and hips. Others are well into high school before people stop assuming they're younger than their sister in seventh grade. From time to time, all of us wonder, *Is this normal?*

All the different body shapes and sizes you see at school, on TV, or in magazines are "normal" for those women (although most magazines use digitally altered photos to make women look perfect, but we'll talk about that later).

On the following pages, we'll tackle the major questions you have about your entry into the land of womanhood, and arm you with tips that'll help you meet all the challenges! So first, let's get right to that fundamental question: "What is normal, anyway?"

Even though many people try to tell you that you have to conform to their rules to be *normal,* normal really can't be the same thing as being *same.* If it were, all the *different* things on this planet would be *abnormal.* (How weird would it be sharing earth with seven billion of your clones?) Everybody's different, and everybody's normal. Some people are normally tall, while others are normally short. Some are normaly small, while others are normally big. (You get the picture.)

So, in the real world, *different* is actually what is *normal.* God created you to be a unique person, and He even put you on a schedule to develop differently than other girls that's just right for you.

Top 10 Questions Teen Girls Ask

We know you have questions. So we came up with a list of the 10 questions girls ask most frequently. We're going to give you the answers, too.

1 — I'm 15 and haven't started my period yet! What's wrong with me?

Physicians tell us that girls can begin their menstrual cycle as early as nine or as late as 17. You'll probably fall somewhere in the middle. If you're really worried about something, you can make an appointment with your family doctor or gynecologist.

2 — Help! My breasts just started developing, they're really sore, and I think my right one is bigger than my left. Am I a freak?

Actually, you're not alone. It may come as a shock, but women's breasts aren't symmetrical—in other words, they don't develop at the same rate. You may feel self-conscious for a while thinking everyone will notice, but the difference is usually so slight, that once you get a bra and clothes on, no one can tell.

The good news is that it won't take long for your breasts to catch up with each other. Just be patient. Many women's breasts are slightly different in size—and you've probably never even noticed.

God Made Us Different

How different are people? Get this: The world is populated with . . .

- five major races (Australoid, Capoid, Caucasian, Oriental, Negro)
- seven colors (black, white, yellow, red, tan, brown, grey)
- 432 major people groups
- 9,000 distinct ethnic groups

Incredible, isn't it? God didn't fill the planet with clones—so why let peer pressure turn you into one?

Here's the most awesome news of all: Despite the billions of men, women, and children who populate earth, Christ shows no favoritism. He loves each one as if they're the only one!

3 I've had my period for almost a year, but I'm very irregular. Sometimes I skip a month, and other times my period lasts for six or seven days. Do I have cancer or something?

During the first couple of years of your menstrual cycle, your body is still adjusting and working out its own schedule. Once again, you're not alone. Thousands of other teen girls have inconsistent periods during the first couple of years.

But if you need a second opinion, schedule an appointment with your family physician or gynecologist.

4 Why am I suddenly getting zits? My face looks like a crater. Is there anything I can do about it?

The very *best* thing you can do is to wash your face twice a day with a gentle face cleanser (not plain soap). Unfortunately, puberty comes right at the height of the teen years—the time most girls are the most self-conscious about changing bodies and hormones. And during this time, your glands are secreting oils, which can build up and cause pimples and acne. The truth is that acne is caused by many different factors besides just oily skin. Not drinking enough water, irritating your skin, fluctuations in your diet, dry weather, really hot weather that causes sweating—all of these things can be factors. A dermatologist can give you a number of different prescriptions that will help according to the type of problem your skin is experiencing.

5

All my friends have boyfriends. I've never had one. What's wrong with me? Am I ugly?

Why do we assume something must be wrong if we don't have a man? Having a boyfriend often has nothing to do with you. It sounds crazy, but sometimes the problem is simply that boys your age don't yet understand the thing that makes you truly attractive and special. Is that your fault? Being yourself sounds cliché, but it really is the best thing you can do to take care of the problem. And if you don't know who "yourself" is, find out! Knowing who you are and what makes you unique is the first priority toward becoming the beautiful creation God intended you to be.

Your differences are your best assets so accentuate them and you'll be well on your way to discovering what really matters to that man you're hoping to find someday.

Don't get me wrong. I completely understand the feeling of wanting to be included and be a part of the fun your friends seem to be having. And it's one of the most difficult things in the world to watch everyone else getting something that you don't. But there's a very real possibility that God is keeping you for Himself. Sound selfish? Maybe. But if you really think about it, what could be better than having the God of the universe single you out for something bigger—a different purpose with a higher calling? He wants to use you for something you can't even imagine and maybe He knows a boyfriend would only distract you from that right now.

At this early stage in your life, relationships are all about looks. But later on, the guy worth your interest will be someone who cares more for your inner beauty than he does your outer beauty. It's true. When you believe you're worth more than a pretty face and a hairstyle, you'll be attracting the kind of guys all your girlfriends are really wishing for.

6 **I think my parents are from another planet. They don't understand me at all! I don't even think they try. I get so frustrated and we're always arguing. What should I do?**

First of all, there is such a thing as "the art of communication." Communicating effectively is tough. And no matter who you're dealing with, *good* communication is a two-way process that requires both parties be willing to say what they mean and mean what they say.

How and when you approach your parents is something to think about it. Your mom comes home from work balancing three bags of groceries, and the minute she steps through the door, you start in with, "How come we never have anything good to eat? I'm starving!" or "Can you drive me to Jamie's tonight?"

Bad timing = bad communication.

What will really get your parents' attention is if you show them how responsible you are. Voluntarily make dinner (even if it's just some sandwiches), or clean up around the house. Believe me, your parents *will* notice! And when they do, your request will sound much more plausible. And sometimes, just waiting for a time that's more convenient can be the very thing that gets your message across. Especially if your message doesn't involve a lot of yelling.

If you provide some time to really sit down and talk with your folks—and no one's angry—you can address and resolve all kinds of issues!

By the way . . . when was the last time you told your parents you love them? (Why not do it now?)

7 **I haven't started dating yet, but when I do, I'm worried that I won't know what to do if and when a guy tries to get me to "go all the way."**

Wise women think ahead. First, be extremely selective about whom you choose to date. Don't go out with a guy just because he asks. Set standards about dating guys who share your faith and your morals, and who respect you. And never date anyone you don't know. Establish a friendship first. And not that a guy you know will never try to get hot and heavy, but chances are *greater* that he won't if he knows you—and knows you know him.

When you accept a date with a friend, he needs to know your standards first off. And then if he tries something you're not comfortable with, you can firmly remind him, "No, I already made it clear that I'm not comfortable with that. Try something like that again, and we're through." You'll want to say it in your own words and make sure he isn't simply trying to reach over you to unlock your door or something. But as you already know, if some guys think they can get away with something, they're definitely going to try. Being prepared and leaving yourself some options is the best thing you can do to ease your mind about dating.

8

This is really embarrassing, but I think something's wrong with me. My vagina is itchy and burns and the discharge smells funny. Is this a yeast infection?

Yep. They're very common and can be treated with over-the-counter medication. But just so you're not assuming anything, make an appointment with your doctor, and let him make a proper diagnosis. For an infection, he'll recommend a cream or gel that will clear it up in about a week.

9

Some of my friends have had a pelvic examination. Do I need one? And what happens during the exam?

Unless you have a specific situation that warrants an exam (like severe cramping that prevents you from your daily routine, or a history of ovarian cancer in your family), it's likely you won't need to have one until your early- or mid-twenties. If you are having PMS symptoms (headaches, cramping, moodiness, hot flashes, nausea) you could consider making an appointment for an exam to go over some options for how to deal with those things. Finding a gynecologist you can trust is of utmost importance.

The best way to find a good gynecologist is to find a woman you trust and ask her if there is a doctor she likes. Short of that, there are many gynecologists listed in the phone book and a quick phone interview with the office staff or a nurse can answer many of your questions before making an appointment.

Something you might want to ask is if it is a law for doctors to have another person present in the room during the exam. While it is law in some states for gynecologists to have another person present, it isn't in all states. Of course, you could ask a good friend or a parent to accompany you. Another consideration is whether the doctor is male or female. Some women prefer to go to a female gynecologist, but male doctors can be just as understanding and often even more willing to ensure you feel comfortable and at ease. The point is to ask all the questions so you will feel as comfortable as possible beforehand. Here are a few considerations before making an appointment for an exam:

• Will the doctor take the time to let you ask questions and not make you feel dumb or embarrassed? Will you feel comfortable in the office/exam room? (The office staff can tell you about the doctor's methods and a quick visit to the doctor's office can also help determine what your comfort level will be.)

• What kind of approach does the doctor have about medications? For example, does he/she consider alternatives like holistic approaches to hormone supplements and antidepressants?

When you do arrive at the doctor's office for your first exam, mention the fact that it is your first exam to the nurse and that you'd like the physician to explain what he or she is going to do first. Before she leaves, you'll be asked to remove your clothing and change into a gown. When the doctor comes into the room, he or she will explain the entire procedure to you.

She'll ask you to lie on the examination table with your feet in special holders called "stirrups" located at the end of the table. This will naturally force your legs apart. With a special instrument inserted into the vagina, she'll take a specimen of cervical tissue with a large cotton swab. It sounds complicated, but it only takes a few seconds. The cotton swab procedure is known as a "pap smear," and the pelvic examination is actually when the doctor presses on your stomach to feel your ovaries for any abnormalities.

If you've been worried about it, there's not a better feeling in the world than knowing you're healthy. It's a quick procedure for your peace of mind!

10 What's a hysterectomy?

Simply put, a hysterectomy is the name for the procedure that removes the female reproductive organs. Some women have a "partial hysterectomy"—removal of the ovaries—for birth control reasons, especially if there is a history of ovarian cancer in the family. A "complete hysterectomy" includes the ovaries and the uterus.

The complete procedure is only used if a woman is at risk for (or has) uterine cancer. With ovarian cancer, or severe endometriosis—thickening of the uterine lining—partial hysterectomy is usually sufficient (although in high risk cases, the complete procedure is often recommended).

But forget all that for now. There's no sense in worrying about cancer, especially at your age. While there have been extremely rare cases of uterine or ovarian cancer in teenagers, it is not common and certainly no one has ever died because she didn't worry enough.

Hormones: The Ride of Your Life

It's a typical day with some typical frustrations. Your hair isn't doing what you want it to, your bagel stayed in the toaster a few seconds too long, and you can't seem to find the disk for your history assignment.

It's a day like any other day, but today, the details seem to be too much to handle. Anxiety starts to creep in. You yell for your little brother to help you search for your disk. He tells you to do it yourself, as usual, and before you know it, you've expressed your true feelings.

"Darin, you twerp! It's probably in that waste pile you call a room!"

"Hey, everybody! Get out of the way! Moody Maggie is on the loose again!"

Does your brother have a special nickname for you a few days out of every month? Some days you seem to start crying at school for no apparent reason, your face breaks out more than usual, you feel unattractive, and you snap at your best friend.

It's a common day all right, but today you're riding the Hormone Highway. Mood swings back and forth and self-esteem bottoms out.

Buckle Up for a Bumpy Ride

Hormones. What are they? And why do they have to invade your body?

When God created females, He gave them specific hormones, biochemical compounds that are manufactured in one part of your body and sent through your bloodstream to another part. Each one brings about various chemical responses. There are hormones inside you that deserve credit for your growth, your metabolic rate, and the physical and emotional changes you experience during puberty. And as you probably already figured out, puberty is that special time of life when you become capable of being a mom (physically at least).

As a girl, your potential to reproduce is announced by your first menstrual period and managed by a complex variety of hormones. Along with those mood managers come a slew of new emotions, grabbing hold of you in the two weeks prior to your period and justifying the clinical designation Premenstrual Syndrome (PMS). You may be irritable, a bit depressed, restless, and have difficulty concentrating for a few days each month.

While they aren't fun destinations, they're likely to be part of your life travels, so buckle up! Take the best course possible with the following tips.

Let God Have the Wheel

The best way to travel the Hormone Highway is with God doing the driving. If you have a regular menstrual cycle, you can look at a calendar and calculate when your moody days will begin. However, if you're like many teen girls, your cycle may be irregular, and the beginning of your cycle may catch you by surprise.

Whatever the case, when you do experience that moment of anxiety, tension, impatience, or low self-esteem, take some time to pray. Say, "God, thanks for making me a girl. You know how I'm feeling right now. Please cause Your love and light to shine through me. Please help me to remember I am created in Your image. Lord, I know Your Spirit will guide me through these days. Let me live in a way that will honor You."

Once you've prayed about your situation, depend on God's strength in every moment. And if you forget for a moment and say or do something you regret, remind yourself to come back and read this again. Pray. Confess your sin if you need to and remember that God will never become tired of hearing from you, His beautiful, uniquely created daughter.

Take the Scenic Route

There's no way to avoid the Hormone Highway. Every girl gets to travel it whether she wants to or not. So instead of complaining about it or dreading it, why not make the best of it?

Here are a few ways to help you appreciate the scenery.

1 **Saturate yourself in God's Word. Start with these Scriptures.**

"Because of the Lord's great love we are not consumed, for his compassions never fail. They are new every morning; great is your faithfulness" (Lamentations 3:22-23).

"Come to me, all you who are weary and burdened, and I will give you rest. Take my yoke upon you and learn from me, for I am gentle and humble in heart, and you will find rest for your souls" (Matthew 11:28-29).

"For you created my inmost being; you knit me together in my mother's womb. I praise you because I am fearfully and wonderfully made; your works are wonderful, I know that full well" (Psalm 139:13-14).

"If anyone speaks, he should do it as one speaking the very words of God. If anyone serves, he should do it with the strength God provides, so that in all things God may be praised through Jesus Christ" (1 Peter 4:11).

2 **Exercise when you know you're becoming moody. Physical activity can help ease tension. Make an effort to take a walk or swim a few laps.**

3 **For the two weeks before your menstrual cycle, try to eat lots of vegetables and drink plenty of water. Also, try to avoid caffeine (coffee, Coke, and chocolate).**

4 **If you're still struggling to appreciate the ride, consider visiting a doctor. Some women use stabilizing medications and you, your parents, and your physician should be able to decide if this is an appropriate option for you.**

You Only Get One Body

We've all seen them on the album covers, in magazines, makeup ads, television commercials, movie previews, billboards, phone booths, newspapers, Internet sites, and grocery store aisles. Who are they? Rail thin models, actresses, and female entertainers who have been surgically enhanced, digitally manipulated, and artistically retouched with the help of an army of professionals and computer technologies. Yeah, they look great. But who are they? Next to the average American woman, these rendered human beings are far from natural. And yet what do they tell us? *Compare your body to this. See if you measure up.*

Do you pass the test? Me neither. But because they're on the cover of a magazine we're supposed to accept that airbrushed babes are what we should be. And all of us are left fighting to fit our less-than-perfect bodies into an unnatural ideal.

Wanting to be fit and feel good about ourselves is the goal. But only when we reject the "ideal" and become motivated to make our bodies honoring to God, can we truly achieve that goal. It will *not* be because you hope to be more popular or more attractive as a skinny mini! Millions of teen girls have bought the lie that they must obtain an unnatural physical image and many of them develop eating disorders as a result.

Time for a reality check? Here's a fact:

The average American woman is 5'4" and weighs 146 pounds (*not* 5'9" and 90 pounds).

And all that statistic really means is that most women are either shorter or taller than that, and weigh more or less than average. The females we see in the beauty and entertainment industries are *not,* I repeat, *not* the average! If you compare yourself to the image of perfection, you will always fall short. There is none perfect; no, not one! Why would you want to be consistently unhappy with the way you look? What a trap! You are beautiful as a unique (and holy!) creation of the One High God who loves you more than anything on earth. He has custom designed the body just for you. Your job is to live in it, keep it healthy, feed it, and exercise it to keep it running well (no pun intended).

So forget the supermodels. Your true "model" is in the way God sees you—perfect, perfect, and *perfect.*

So without further ado, here are our 10 "model" tips to get you the best body possible!

1 Use the FDA Food Pyramid.

You know: that pyramid that tells you what and how much to eat (you'll find it at the end of the book). Use the pyramid to evaluate whether you are eating the right foods and the right amounts of those foods to provide your body with the fuel it needs to function at its best. Start at the bottom of the pyramid and work your way up. The foods in the lower levels are typically low-fat, low-calorie, high fiber, and high in nutrients. The bulk of your diet should come from those levels. As you move up, the portions become smaller and fewer. Eating a variety of foods each day (and taking a multi-vitamin) will help you get the healthy stuff your body needs.

2 Go for the Grains!

Your body needs six to 11 servings per day, depending on your normal weight. A serving could be one slice of whole grain bread (wheat, rye, barley), 1/2 cup of cooked brown rice, oatmeal, or pasta, or one cup of whole grain cereal. Carbohydrates are energy, and fiber keeps things moving through the pipes at a good pace. Try it and see if you don't stay awake better during seventh period!

3. Major in Fruits and Veggies.

The key to healthy cell development and higher energy levels is to eat three to five raw fruits and at least two cups of raw vegetables every day. The key word is raw, as in uncooked and loaded with living enzymes. Overcooked veggies have the nutrition zapped right out of them. They are still a better choice than a cupcake or a bowl of Velveeta, but fresh and raw—or even lightly steamed—is best. So sprinkle some zesty seasonings on that steamed broccoli or cauliflower and give your mouth time to learn to like it. Pretty soon, you won't even remember why you ever liked all those processed, packaged foods.

4. It Does a Body Good.

It's easy to get the calcium you need with bone-strengthening dairy products like a cup of skim or soy milk, 1/2 cup nonfat yogurt, or low-fat cottage cheese (though cheese should be an occasional treat due to its high-fat content). Soy and dairy products also contain protein for strong muscles, so you can steer clear of red meat entirely if you like. Two to three servings (a serving is about the size of your fist) of grilled or broiled chicken, turkey, fish, beans, peas, or eggs are all excellent protein sources as well. Protein bars and drinks are good sources as well, as are nuts, but these shouldn't be your main protein source.

5   Trash the Tasty Temptations.

Those high-fat, high-sugar treats that make you weak in the knees can also weaken your body! Yes, we *need* some fat in our diets, so good fats like olive oil, avocados, and almonds are good in small doses. Other fats should be limited to very small servings—two teaspoons per day of butter, mayonnaise, cream cheese, or sour cream. And that doesn't mean two of each. Sweeten foods with honey, pure maple syrup, fruit juice, or other natural sweeteners like fructose (available at health food stores). Forget artificial sweeteners like saccharin. Here's where the rubber meets the road: Fast food, pizza, frozen dinners, peanut butter, jelly, pies, whipped cream, donuts, cookies, candy, ice cream, cakes—basically all the items that make you salivate to read about—are all treats and shouldn't be part of your daily habit. Remember, you're choosing body health over momentary pleasure! Develop good eating habits and your battle for health will be a piece of cake (sorry).

Next time you pull up to that drive-through window, choose chicken over a burger, a veggie over a beef burrito, pancakes over breakfast sandwiches, veggie pizza over triple meat with extra cheese—are you getting the picture?—juice over soda, a muffin over cheesecake . . . you'll be well on your way to the healthy body God intended for you. You can also check restaurant chains and your local library for fast-food nutritional guides.

6   Make Educated Nutritional Decisions.

Do you really need that chocolate bar? Actually, you might. If you're one of the women who has this common craving, you could have a natural serotonin deficiency (a hormone that controls happiness) of which chocolate is a big provider. But generally when you get the munchies, chocolate belongs in the "special occasion" category. Snacks like sugar-free smoothies, fresh fruit, pretzels, baked potato chips, rice cakes, air-popped popcorn, fruit bars, fat-free pudding, or carrot and celery sticks are your boring options here. But there are lots of things you can do to spruce up even the healthiest diet. All you have to do is start finding them.

7 Make Fitness a Priority.

Lace up your shoes and don that sports bra because it's time to strengthen your heart, lungs, muscles, and mind with a great aerobic workout. Aerobic exercise involves the entire body and requires that the heart rate be elevated for at least 30 minutes before results begin to show. Start with a two- to four-minute warm-up (this will raise your internal temperature, warming your muscles to improve your performance and prevent injury). Then increase the intensity for about 20 minutes, and follow with a cool-down period of five to seven minutes. Be creative by varying your exercise so you won't get bored and be tempted to quit. Try brisk walking, jogging, skating, cycling, dancing, jumping rope, trampolines, basketball, swimming, kick-boxing, or get an aerobic video from the library and give that a try!

8 Incorporate Your Training Zone.

Get the most out of your workout by checking your heart rate several times to see if you are within your target zone. Locate your pulse on your wrist or the side of your neck. Count the number of beats in six seconds, then multiply by 10. A safe training rate for teens is about 120-180 beats per minute. If you are under that, you need to work harder. If you are over, slow down. Let your body be your guide. For best results, work out four to six times per week. For faster results, work out longer not harder! And always stay in your training zone.

9   Maintain an Active Lifestyle.

You don't need to take time out of your day when you make exercise a way of life. That way, you won't to be tempted to cut corners on your workout. Try riding your bike to school or rollerblading to a friend's house instead of driving. Take the stairs instead of the escalator or the elevator. Do some leg lifts while you're on the phone or while blow-drying your hair. Just don't go overdoing it: Remember your goal is to have the body God intended you to have—not get on the cover of *Fit* magazine.

10   Stay Balanced.

The Bible encourages us to do things in moderation. It's easy to go overboard with exercise or be too strict with your diet if you're focused on the wrong goal. Pretty soon, life will lose its fun. On the other hand, eating everything you want all the time and never working out is just begging for problems. When you are working toward a healthier you, you will have a happier attitude and a better outlook on life. Eating well and getting regular exercise helps you get there!

Bloomin' Groomin'

Every morning when the sun comes up and presents you with a new day, it's a new opportunity to present your best self to the world! Well, okay, probably not to the *whole* world, but at least family, friends, classmates, teachers—people like that. To help you make your best impression, here're some tips on common areas of your daily grooming procedure. Follow these simple steps and you'll have no problem knocking off some socks!

Hose Yourself Down

Actually, if you don't have a hose, a regular ol' shower will do the trick. Roll yourself out of those comfy sheets, grab a fluffy towel, and let that H$_2$O flow from head to toe! Lather up a washcloth or nylon scrubby with shower gel or your favorite bar of mild soap and pay some extra attention to the odorous areas of your bod. Daily showers are especially important during menstruation.

Depending on whether your hair is naturally dry or oily, you'll probably need to shampoo at least every other day. Short hair tends to need it more often. With conditioner, every few days is fine, and only near the ends! Too much conditioner can make your hair feel heavy and look oily and dull. So, don't overdo it.

Select a razor with a solid grip, a swivel head with two or three blades, and a moisturizing strip. These features will help reduce nicks and cuts. Suds up and shave in the direction of the hair growth, and then against it (that would be down, then up). Shaving creams or gels with vitamin E or aloe provide extra soothing of the skin.

Maximize your femininity by minimizing rough skin. Put an end to dry or rough patches on heels, ankles, and elbows with a pumice stone or loofah. Do this while your skin is already wet. Work the stone or scrub in a circular motion and watch the dead skin cells slough right off. And while your skin is still warm and damp, moisturize. The lotion will seal in your skin's natural moisture leaving it feeling soft and supple.

Did you notice your body has begun to perspire and smell? When perspiration mixes with bacteria, we get body odor. Naturally, showering washes much of it away, but using an antiperspirant deodorant will take care of the rest. Most products are two-in-one, meaning they contain a deodorant to stop odor and an antiperspirant to stop wetness. You may or may not need both. But you can probably figure out what you need if you pay attention to your body.

Mouth Matters

People will enjoy your beautiful smile when you can flash it with confidence. And what a confident smile you flash when you have sparkling teeth and fresh breath. After each meal, and especially after eating sweets, brush your teeth, tongue, gums, and even the roof of your mouth. Use a soft bristle brush recommended by your dentist and turn the bristles to a 45 degree angle. The inside of your front teeth can then be brushed up and down, using your toothbrush vertically. Don't neglect your molars way in the back.

A spin brush or a sonic toothbrush can get you even cleaner teeth. But remember to be gentle on your gums. You can actually wear away gum tissue if you're too aggressive or use a brush that's too hard.

Flossing can be a chore, but when you get good at it, it will take only about two minutes out of your day. Along with that, mouthwash can be added to your daily routine if you want extra protection from Mr. Yuck Mouth.

Model Skin Care and Makeup

Now that you're clean, it's time to take care of your features with cosmetics that appear natural, not made-up. I've worked with some talented makeup artists, and collected quite a few tips and tricks of the trade to share. These are the simple, but totally sensational secrets from the pros.

First, identify your skin type. Take this simple test: Before you turn out the lights and call it a night, cleanse your face. Do not apply anything to your skin (no astringent, no lotion). The next day as soon as you wake up, lay a small piece of tissue paper over your entire face. Now press the tissue against your skin at your forehead, cheeks, sides of your nose, and middle of your chin. Now lift the tissue, holding it up to the light. A slight bit of oil indicates normal skin, no oil means you have dry skin, lots of oil is a sure sign of oily skin. If you are oily in one spot and dry in another, you are the proud owner of very common combination skin. Actually, most teens are oily in the "T-zone"—across the forehead and down the center of the face.

Carefully read labels and choose products for your skin type. When it comes to skin care, use products from the same company because they have been designed to work together. Look for allergy-tested, fragrance-free, non-comedogenic (won't clog pores).

Keeping your skin fresh and clear requires double duty. Cleanse your face with a non-detergent bar, lotion, or gel once in the morning and once in the evening (never go to bed with your makeup on!). Work up a sudsy lather while moving your fingertips in a circular motion. Your facial skin and muscles are very delicate so avoid pulling, rubbing, or pressing hard! Remove the cleanser using lukewarm water, then gently pat dry with a clean towel.

Next, dab some astringent or toner on a fluffy 100 percent cotton ball, and apply it to your face. Use circular motions all the way up to your hairline and under your chin, steering clear of your eye area. Astringent or toner will help to slough off dead skin cells (technically known as exfoliation) and remove excess oil.

Last but not least, treat your skin with moisturizer. This will seal in natural fluids and replace moisture your skin loses due to sun, wind, perspiration, air conditioning or heating, and pollution. All skin types need moisture. Normal to dry skin requires a heavier one, normal to oily skin should go with an oil-free type. And don't forget your precious lips! Lip balm softens and prevents chapping. And you can even choose one in your favorite flavor like cherry, wild berry, or orange.

TLC for Your Skin

Try these tips to make your skin feel special:

- Drink six to eight glasses of water each day to cleanse your skin from the inside out. And, no: sodas and lattes don't count!

- Apply an SPF 15 or higher sunscreen every day to protect your skin. A lot of moisturizers and foundations already have sunscreen in them.

- Once or twice a week, open up your pores with a bowl of steam or by pressing a wet, warm washcloth against your face for two to four minutes. Then splash with warm water—about 10 times. Now apply a facial scrub to chase away any dull-looking skin. Choose one made with soft exfoliaters—no ground up fruit pits! Rinse well and apply a toner.

- Most acne is treatable. When you have an acne attack switch to a cleanser or toner that contains salicylic acid. A product with benzoyl peroxide directly kills bacteria in the zit to speed up the healing process. If these over-the-counter zit-zappers don't cut it, find a dermatologist.

Makeup Magic

It might seem hard to imagine, but when models are out of the limelight, they wear very little makeup. Skin needs a chance to breathe and the natural look is definitely the best. So here are the "barely there" makeover techniques that work. Remember that less is best. Let it be your bright eyes and sparkling smile that others notice about you, not your wild eyeliner or lip color.

1 If you choose to wear foundation to even out your skin tone, select a lightweight formula. Match it to your skin tone by dabbing a bit on your jawline. If it blends in, go with it. Use a cosmetic sponge to apply it evenly to your entire face including your eyelids and your lip line, blending at your jaw line (not on your neck). Wipe off any excess on eyebrows. Follow with a light dusting of translucent face powder to set the foundation. Just don't overdo it.

2 If you are skipping foundation, start with a shade of powder that is closest to your skin tone. Use loose powder or pressed powder with a brush to avoid the caked look sometimes caused by the powder-puff pad.

3 Sweep blush across your cheeks in an upward movement. Blush should go no further in toward your nose than the center of your eye, no lower than the bottom of your nose. Light- and medium-toned skins can select a neutral tone like mocha pink. Dark-skinned girls can handle a deeper shade like berry or plum. This will minimize the contrast between your skin tone and blush color, which adds to a natural look. Add too much? Rather than trying to wipe it off, simply tone it down by applying a light dusting of translucent face powder over the top.

4 Now it's time to define your eyes and thicken your lashes. First, apply a light shade of eye shadow over your entire eyelid. Apply a medium tone from the center of your eyelid to the outer corner, extending the shadow up into your crease. Blend well.

Second, using a soft-kohl eye pencil in a color that matches your lashes (brown, brown-black, or charcoal), apply the liner directly against your lashes making the outer corners a bit thicker. Shaky hand? Make a row of dots then connect them with a sponge-tip or cotton-tip applicator.

Third, it's mascara time. Coat the tips of your lashes using the tip of the mascara wand. Wait 30 seconds then coat your entire lashes working the wand bristles into your lashes for great coverage. To apply mascara to bottom lashes, tip your chin down, looking up into the mirror. Come up underneath lashes. Use an eyelash comb to separate stuck-together lashes.

5 Finish your look with lovely lips. Have fun with your glosses and lipsticks. For longer lasting color, use a lip pencil to line your lips, then fill it in. Now top it off with a light- to medium-toned gloss. Steer clear of dark tones that will make lips look small or from reds that can make a girl look like she's playing dress up.

Now all you need is a friendly smile because *you* are a model too. Every day you model Christ to other teens who need to know Him. Show them how great it is to have a Savior who wants to bless their lives and get them through the tough stuff of life. Wow! Now that's being a model!

The Savvy Shopper

Becca, Holly, Kristen, and LaKesha had plans to go shopping Tuesday after class. They'd all decided to help Becca hunt down the perfect outfit for the coming weekend—Saturday night dinner at Becca's mom's boss's house, Mr. Hansen. Not only did she want to impress Mr. and Mrs. Hansen, they also had a son her age who was totally hot. So, of course, Becca had to find just the right outfit.

At 3:23 they reached their destination, and the four girls headed directly for the junior department where tight, ribbed midriffs and low-cut hip-huggers waited.

When Becca emerged from the dressing room modeling her selection, she was met with conflicting expressions. Holly thought the ensemble was perfect, especially at the bargain price. Kristen didn't think it was "classic" enough, whatever that meant. And LaKesha was concerned that Becca's parents might not be down with the style.

But feeling daring, Becca decided that at this price, she could afford to be a little adventurous. A bold outfit was exactly the thing she needed so she surprised them all by buying it.

When she came downstairs Saturday night, not only did her dad freak when he saw her, but suddenly Becca wasn't feeling quite as brave as she had back in the store with her friends. The two-piece ensemble suddenly looked more like something Holly would wear, not her. And the fact that it had been on sale was no consolation now. What in the world was she going to do?

Sound familiar? We've all made some careless fashion decisions. But a closet full of clothes and nothing to wear doesn't have to be the norm.

Learning the art of savvy shopping will save you time, money, and embarrassment. It will also bring you one step closer to being a Proverbs 31 woman: She searches for super buys and thinks about it before she pays. She is *not* an impulse shopper. She asks herself: Do I need this? Is this worth the money? Do I already own something similar to this?

Try these tips to help you make better clothing decisions and spend less time standing in the closet with nothing to wear.

• Be a Copycat Shopper.

That means study the popular brands and the designer lines so you can find look-alikes for half the cost. With many lines you are paying extra money for the name on the label. Forget that! Go for well-made items at moderate prices.

• Shop for Quality, Not Quantity.

Your shopping goal should be to keep things as simple as possible—don't just load up your closet with clothes. With lower-quality clothes you may be able to stretch your dollar but chances are they won't hold up. Do a quality check on the buttons, zippers, seams, and top-stitching.

• Check Your Mood.

In a wild and crazy mood? Be careful not to buy something you'll never be brave enough to wear in public. The opposite can also be true. If you are feeling down or lonely, you might be tempted to go for something you don't need in dark colors that you won't even want once your funk has passed. So know how you feel, and buy when you feel like *yourself!*

• Know a Timeless Classic from a Flashy Fad.

Classic style clothes are usually tailored and timeless, meaning they don't go in and out of fashion. For instance, five-pocket jeans, turtlenecks, cardigans, straight cut skirts—these are always in style. Classics make the best investments. Fads are unique or funky styles that are hot for a short time, but once that time is over, you wouldn't want to be caught anywhere in them! To avoid wasting money on fads, simply purchase one or two fads each season. But keep in mind that just because a look is popular doesn't mean you should wear it. Some trendy clothes are totally inappropriate for women who want to honor the Lord with their bodies. Modesty is the key. So skip the low-cut tops, the hipster denims, the lacy and sheer fabrics. Choose to be a princess, because after all, you're a daughter of the King!

• Plan Ahead with Prints and Polka Dots.

If you like clothes with flower prints or bold stripes or traditional plaids, keep in mind that you can't wear them all together! As a general rule (and especially with a limited budget) choose solid bottoms (pants, skirts, shorts) and printed tops or vice versa! FYI . . . keep in mind that horizontal stripes add width and vertical patterns add height. Solid colors from top to bottom make a body look taller. Use these tips to your best advantage.

• Be Color Conscious.

Choose three to five colors that make you look and feel your best. When you purchase tops and bottoms in these hues (or in ones that coordinate with them) you will automatically expand your wardrobe. This gives you mix 'n' matchability! It is also helpful to shop for complete outfits rather than buying one piece at a time. That way you won't have to worry about buying something to match later.

• Know When Enough Is Enough.

Don't overbuy on the same item. You probably don't need seven pairs of jeans, especially when you're going to a dress-up event and have no nice pants. Create a well-rounded wardrobe so you will have the right outfit for every occasion from school to church to a night out to a wedding.

- **Approach Sale Racks with Caution.**

What appears to be a bargain may not be. Ask yourself: Is this item on the sale rack because it's not made well, or because it's off-colored, damaged, or going out of style? Does this fabric require expensive dry cleaning?

Occasionally you really can get great deals, but always check the tag before purchasing from the sale rack!

- **Buy Clothes with One or Two Trusted Friends.**

Group shopping is perfect when you're just cruising the mall for fun. But it is too difficult to make savvy shopping decisions when everyone is giving you their opinions. No doubt, some will like the outfit and some won't. So on those serious shopping sprees limit it to someone whose opinion you trust.

Part Two Dating & Relating

The Inside Scoop on Guys

Note: This chapter is written by a P.E. teacher and coach who also happens to be a guy. We figured since he's been one all his life and he's around guys all the time, he'd probably have a good idea of how guys think and feel. Check it out!

Guys. You can't avoid them. They're all over the place. You go to school with them, work with them, and live near them. Some even choose to date them. Sometimes they're exactly who and what you need them to be. And other times they can be real jerks. They frustrate you, and sometimes you're tempted to just give up on them entirely. They're all so *typical*—and yet so *different*. So how can you know what any of them are thinking at all?

You've probably already figured out that guys are waaay different from girls. But they're not simply different on the outside; they're different inside too. No doubt you've noticed that guys think and react to things in very different ways than girls. To get an idea of what makes guys guys, it probably couldn't hurt to take a look at life from a guy's perspective.

At the basic guy level, there are three main statements that describe most guys. Knowing them in advance will help you get a head start in understanding the male species. So if you haven't been taking notes, you might want to start now.

1 Guys are all about the eyes.

When guys see something they like, they're attracted to it. It could be a motorcycle, a big, juicy steak, or a cool jacket. A guy will see a car commercial and think, *Wow. That's a great looking car. I want it.* A girl might see the same commercial and think: *I wonder if the seats are comfy. Does it have a CD player?* And you can be sure those little fold-down visor mirrors were not invented for guys to check their makeup. All a guy cares about is that the car *looks* good—and how good he'd probably look driving it.

The first thing a guy notices is a girl's looks. Of course, I'm speaking in general terms: No two guys are alike. But most guys—even Christian guys—are initially attracted by sight. It's just natural for a guy to think about physical appearance because God created males to be this way.

A guy's not going to be turned on (at least initially) by the fact that you make good grades, are organized, or can bake a mean green bean casserole. Sure, these things are important to many guys, but they just don't always care about all that right away. *Could she be mistaken for a supermodel?* That's a little closer to what the typical guy is thinking.

So now that you're completely depressed . . . Understand that this is no excuse for guys who act like jerks, and that the ones who place major significance on a girl's looks are super shallow, emotionally immature, and extremely shallow. Did I say shallow twice? I meant to say it three times.

But as an eligible female, you're likely to come into contact with at least a few of these guys. Luckily, God made you more emotionally developed at a younger age than He made the guys, so you'll have an advantage in knowing how to handle it.

So how do you know if a guy *feels* anything for you besides that physical attraction? How do you know you're going to get an intelligent conversation out of him and know he's genuinely caring? Read on.

2 Guys are physical.

Ever since they were little boys, most guys have really enjoyed activities that involve physicality. That's why sports and getting in fights and touching girls are such important things to them.

Ready to get blunt here? A guy may be the nicest person you've met, but he'll still want to hold your hand, kiss you, hold you, and have sex with you. When a guy kisses a girl, it feels good. It gives him all these amazing senses and thoughts. To the girl, it's a *soul* thing—a symbol of commitment, an example of deep connection, a promise that he wants to know you better and maybe even loves you. Not that girls don't enjoy the physical feeling too, but for the guy, a kiss is probably just the first stop on the highway to heavier action. Whatever it makes him feel emotionally or spiritually, he's thinking of the physical first and foremost. Once again, it's the way God made him, but God also gave him self-control. It's no excuse for taking advantage.

3 Guys are aggressive.

Okay? This isn't astrophysics. One thought back to your fifth grade P.E. class should remind you: When you saw guys playing dodge ball, did they give it a light toss, or did they chuck it with the force of a Sherman tank cannon? Thought so. Maybe they don't play dodge ball anymore, but the aggression part doesn't really change. The fact is, guys are usually the sexual aggressor in a relationship. God made them that way too. Just as He made you to be caring and nurturing, He made guys to be aggressive.

But again, this doesn't mean you have to let him act on that right now. Let's backtrack for a sec. Remember a minute ago I said guys like to kiss and hug because it feels good? They like the physical rush . . . but the emotional part often isn't as important to them. Know why? Most teen guys are incapable of handling an emotional and spiritual connection.

If a guy ever says, "I love you, and having sex with you is one way I can show you how much," cut him loose. Not only is he selfish and unrepentant about it, he doesn't even care what your interests in the matter are. He can't! He doesn't have the mental capacity or responsibility to care and provide for you— much less love you.

What's the Answer?

Group dating really is the best (and safest) way to go. It has so many positives, first of all, because it takes all the pressure off! You don't feel as though you're on display or being taken for a test drive. It allows you to see your date interact with others and learn about his character. And if the conversation with him starts to lag . . . hey, you've got your girlfriends there! But the best thing is, you're not alone with a guy in a car or somewhere which is just unsafe and uncomfortable.

If you allow yourself to be alone with a guy, he tends to interpret that as a "go ahead" and it can be difficult to change his mind. Make the message clear from the beginning, so there won't be any confusion.

Here's some advice about using e-mail: Never type anything you wouldn't want everybody to see. The same can be said for dating. Don't say or do anything with a guy that you wouldn't want everybody to see. God is going to see it anyway, and that should be enough.

And speaking of God, what does *He* have to do with this subject? Well, He created you and He loves you more than you can imagine! And since He has your best interests at heart, you can trust Him with your life. Can you believe that He really is big enough to bring the right man into your life at the right time?

The thing to remember is that His timing can be (and usually is) different from ours. Consider this: Your whole life is a journey, mapped out by your heavenly Father. Yes, He allows you to make choices about the things you'll do and places you'll go. But His concern is that you're able to take your time and do the things that make your life a complete and rewarding one. As long as you seek Him first and develop a close relationship with Him, the ride should be fulfilling—even through the rough spots.

Take your eyes off God, and you'll miss parts of the journey that He intended for you to see. And when you're more focused on a relationship with a guy than you are on the one with your heavenly Father, there will be gaps in the lifelong trip that you'll never be able to experience again.

And of course, before even *thinking* about a relationship with a guy, make time to fully develop an intimate relationship with Jesus Christ.

Final thought

Two main words of what we've been talking about are *dating* and *waiting*. For some people, dating means looking around for the right guy. Along the way, there's heartache, frustration, rejection, dishonesty, emotional ups and downs, and a lot of wasted time. But with waiting, there's trusting God and His timing.

A godly man of integrity is worth waiting for. A man who adores and respects you, builds you up and accepts you as you are, that's a man worth waiting for! And you know something? God will reveal that man to you in *His time*.

Meanwhile, why not write a letter to your future husband? Even though you don't know who he is yet, God does. And while you're at it, pray that God will let him know you're waiting for him. Pray he'll grow spiritually. Someday you'll have the opportunity to present that to him. Can you imagine how he'll feel when he reads that?

What Language Is That?

With guys and girls both created in the image of God, it's funny how differently they talk and relate. When girls are together, they can chat a mile a minute, sharing details from just about any area of life. When guys are together, they talk about video games, movies, cars, and music. The two approaches to communication are very different.

Things get really interesting, however, when you have a guy and girl standing face-to-face, trying to communicate. She's going on about her feelings, and he's talking about the facts. It might be the same topic, but little understanding is going on.

So what can you do? How can a girl communicate with a guy?

Communication Tips

First, remember who you are. As a Christian, you are a daughter of the King. You have great value and worth. No one is better (or worse) than you. You can hold a conversation with anyone you want. There's no reason to be intimidated.

Second, remember that guys mature slower emotionally than girls. You might meet a guy who can spit out a few worthwhile sentences. But you'll also run into some who don't seem to catch on at all.

Third, remember that a conversation works when you're showing interest in the other person. Ask questions to get the conversation going, throw in your own thoughts, and follow up with more questions. Talking, listening, and understanding happen on a two-way street. Verbal communication isn't usually high on a guy's list of favorite activities, so if you hog the conversation, he's probably going to lose interest fast. Be willing to share your thoughts and opinions, but relax and let him engage once in a while too.

Fourth, treat him as a friend and don't overanalyze. It's normal to think about every possible angle after you talk to a guy. *He talked to me—he must like me! I wonder what he meant by _____. Maybe he meant he likes me!* Do yourself and the guy a favor and leave the questions unanswered for a while. After all, the best relationships are built on friendships. Focus on being a true friend and just try to enjoy your talks with guys like you enjoy chatting with your girlfriends.

A good rule to remember is that guys like girls who are real. If you attempt a conversation with a guy and it goes absolutely nowhere, don't sweat it. Keep being yourself and you're bound to run into a guy who will notice how fun you are to talk with!

Dating or Courtship?

You've probably heard something about it: the debate over which approach to relationships is better. Maybe you've even chosen to go with one side or the other. We have *Brio* readers who fall on both sides—and everywhere in between—of the debate over dating versus courtship.

In our culture, dating has become the standard practice: you know, the "dinner and a movie" thing. The guy gets up the nerve, stutters out an invitation to "go out or something" on Friday, and scampers off before you have time to change your mind. Friday comes and he picks you up in mom's minivan. During the date, you're trying to figure out what he's thinking, and it seems he's doing the same. As he drives you home, you're both way too nervous to act normal, but somehow you manage to get out that you had fun and you hope you can do it again sometime. He pulls up to the curb in front of your house and you open the door before he has time to wonder about a good-night kiss. You close the door and thank him—"see ya Monday"—and scurry up to your front door.

Sure, some of the common elements change: where he's taking you, what he's driving, what outfit you decide on. But the basic premise is the same: Two nervous people try to act as though they're not nervous at all and pretend they've done this a thousand times. And sooner or later, both sides wonder if there's something more developing in the relationship.

Courtship has come to be seen as "anti-dating." Though it has many variations from strict to lenient, basic courtship usually implies that there will be no one-on-one interaction. Group activities and chaperoned outings take the place of solitary dating, and exclusive relationships don't happen between a male and female until engagement. There is generally a higher level of involvement and accountability from mature adults, parents, and friends, and an agreed-upon standard for physical affection.

A common goal of courtship is that before you spend time with a guy, your parents and friends get to know him better first. Thoughts and feelings about faith, family, goals, interests, plans, and pursuits are shared not simply between a guy and a girl, but between families and friends as well.

It can be an intimidating proposal, but the proponents of courtship say that it helps in keeping the goal of relationships in mind and the standards of purity established.

Decisions, Decisions

So does dating dominate courtship or does courtship conquer dating? There are pros and cons to both sides that you and your parents should decide together. Keep in mind that there are godly girls and guys who choose dating, and that courtship doesn't necessarily make relationship-building a more positive experience in and of itself.

Whatever you and your parents think, the issue is important enough to spend some serious time thinking and praying over it. Your parents and you will have ideas about where to set the standards, and all of you will likely have to compromise to arrive at a conclusion. Keep in mind that while it is your life and your future you're dealing with, God gave you these people to help you make such difficult decisions. Your personality, your strengths and weaknesses, your maturity level, and many other factors make a big difference in the decision.

And often, it takes older, more experienced people to help you see yourself for who you really are. Many families find that dating vs. courtship is an issue to continually revisit as new ideas and situations come up. By looking at the pros and cons together and keeping an eye on where God is leading you, you can influence the decision with maturity and wisdom.

Goals with Guys

No matter what route you take, there are some basic goals you'll want to consider as you begin investing in relationships with guys:

• God First

Staying focused in all your relationships is top priority. The danger of forgetting the central component of every true relationship is an ever-present reality. Yet it happens every day. Put simply, if a love interest is causing you to forget your promise to Jesus, you can't afford to continue that relationship.

• Purity

Impurity is more than just a forbidden fruit—it's a life changer. No other decision could be responsible for so many broken hearts and wasted dreams than the decision to throw away purity before being united in total commitment through marriage. The idea to stay as far away from the edge of that boundary as you can isn't just about protecting your body. It's about not wasting the fragile gift God entrusted to you as His child. You see, purity is something we all start with. When people don't accept the responsibility that comes with that gift—to cherish and respect it—disappointment is the inevitable result. In committing to protect the purity you've been given, you make a promise to God, the guy, your family, his family, his future wife, your future husband, and yourself, that you won't be the one to disregard your responsibility. You will uphold your end of the bargain to guard purity.

• Friendship

God has placed great importance on relationships. In Matthew 22:37-40 (NKJV), Jesus told the Pharisees that "all the Law" depended on two commandments: "You shall love the Lord your God with all your heart, with all your soul, and with all your mind," and "You shall love your neighbor as yourself." Friendship is the result of that second commandment. For most of us, we will be lucky to have one or two friends in our lives who loves us as she loves herself. Striving for this kind of love is a chance to reflect God's love for us. The best marriages are built on a solid foundation of friendship.

• Fun

What's "fun" to you? Is it hanging out with a bunch of friends? Or maybe it's that nervous date scenario described earlier. When you've got a relationship with a guy, group activities can add an element of fun and help you both see each other for who you really are. Besides that, they keep the pressure low, let you get to know and interact in many different situations, and just plain multiply the possibilities for fun.

Surviving a Crush

The guy may change, but the feelings are usually the same. Whether he's your brother's best friend, your chemistry lab partner, your English teacher, or a guy who doesn't even know you're alive, it's easy for a girl to have a crush. The hard part can be surviving it.

What's the Deal?

Why does it happen over and over? Why does a guy catch your eye, stay in your mind, and mess with your heart—sometimes without ever speaking a word to you? Because you're human. Because you're a girl. Because it's completely normal.

A girl's mind and heart can be attracted to a guy for all kinds of reasons. Maybe he's cute, maybe he plays in a band, maybe he's the smartest guy in your math class, maybe he carries himself with confidence, maybe he's a godly Christian. The reasons you have a crush on someone can be completely shallow or filled with great insight. Whatever the case, a crush is a crush and not a full-fledged, official relationship, so you need to handle things carefully.

What to Do?

If you have a slight crush on a guy friend— thinking that he's really cute, smart, or cool—you may not need to do much at all. Enjoy the nice feeling you have when you see him, have fun talking with him, and do your best to be a true friend to him.

*If your crush scenario is more serious—*if you think about a guy constantly, if you talk with him in your daydreams but not in person, if you don't really *know* him—you need to start with prayer.

Ask God to ground your thoughts in reality and to direct your mind toward things that are true, good, pure, and trustworthy. Whenever you start dwelling on your crush, send a prayer to God and ask for help in thinking about something else.

The basis of any lasting relationship is truth. A serious crush doesn't provide truth; instead, it gives a false reality. Maybe you've experienced this before when you tried talking to your crush. Once you've had a conversation or two with him, the feelings in your heart can drift back to reality once you see what the guy is really like.

If your crush involves someone who's a few years older, ask God to give you eyes and a heart for someone else—particularly Him. As a teen, you need to have relationships with guys your age before moving on. Later in life you will have relationships with men, but at this point in your life, age really makes a difference.

If your crush involves a married man, don't beat yourself up with guilt. It's common for a girl to have a crush on a man who's a kind authority in her life. It could be a good opportunity to analyze what it is about him that attracts you. Does he have some qualities you have on your list of things you desire your future husband to have? Still, the man you're projecting onto belongs to someone else so don't take your feelings too seriously. Ask God to help you see through it as quickly as possible.

Reprioritize the important things in your life. If right now, your being with a married man seems to be a priority, you need a reality check, sister. Pray, read your Bible, talk to a trusted female adult, whatever. When you start thinking about him, pray and force your mind onto something else—start a project, clean your room, read a book, talk to a friend, etc.

If your crush involves someone you'll probably never meet, such as a movie star or musician, don't worry too much about it. Just be sure your crush doesn't become an obsession. Remember, a Christian's life revolves around Jesus, not any other created thing—which includes cute famous guys.

Crush—What It Says Is What It Does

At some point, every crush ends in reality. Either your crush develops into a real relationship or it doesn't. The chances of things turning out the way you've dreamed are slim—leaving you crushed. That may sound harsh, but it's true.

Be prepared for a few tears and some sadness when it finally sinks in that your crush isn't going to share your feelings, and then do whatever it takes to move on.

God is good. He has good things planned for your life—things you probably can't even imagine! Trust Him with everything, even your crushes. He will be faithful and will provide what (and who) you need when you need it.

What's the Point?

So there's this guy... He's fun, good looking, spiritually strong, and a pretty good friend. You love hanging out with him, and he thinks he'd like to move things on to a deeper level. So how do you really feel about that?

It sounds as though you've got a good thing going. You know each other well. You have fun hanging out; there's none of that awkwardness of "going together." And you're learning how good guys think and behave.

But have you asked yourself "the questions"?

- *Why* do we really want things to become exclusive?

- *How* would it improve things?

- *What* do we want to get out of this relationship?

- *When* could we conceivably move on to marriage?

- *Where* do we see things heading if we don't take this step?

Even after you've answered those questions, you can have trouble knowing what you should do. So how can you really know when you should or shouldn't pursue a deeper relationship with a guy?

First, check out your motives:

- Do you secretly hope that having this guy as a boyfriend might make you more popular?

- Would your friends think you were crazy if you didn't want him as a boyfriend?

- Are you scared you might lose him if you don't accept the title of "girlfriend"?

- Are you curious about starting a physical relationship?

- Are you hoping that this might be a good way to get back at your parents for something?

Fear, rebellion, hormones, curiosity, peer pressure, and popularity are not good reasons to deepen a relationship. Doing so for any of these reasons is actually likely to damage the good relationship you had going.

Next, take some time to examine his motives: Do fears, rebelliousness, hormones, curiosity, peer pressure, or popularity factor in to his thinking? It may be hard for you to determine this on your own, so get some opinions from other people you trust before you decide.

Is Chivalry Dead?

According to Merriam-Webster's, chivalry is the qualities of gallant or distinguished gentlemen. These days, words like "gallant" and "distinguished" and "gentlemen" aren't descriptions of many teen guys. Back in the old days, when a guy wanted to spend time with a young lady, he'd have to get permission from her father. He'd treat her with respect and make sure he never took advantage of the situation. He'd hold doors open for her and pull out her chair for her.

Well, that's nice, you say. *I've been nearly run over by guys trying to get in the cafeteria line ahead of me!*

They're not exactly the shining example of class and charm, are they? What's happened?

Is chivalry in the twenty-first century dead?

What Are class and charm?

Let's start with what chivalry *isn't*. It *isn't* knocking you down to get in front of you in the cafeteria line. It *isn't* trying to impress you with facts like that he hasn't washed his hair in a month.

A guy with class will introduce himself to you, ask about things that are pertinent to your life, and demonstrate that he understands that there's a difference between guys and girls. Unfortunately, again, many guys haven't figured any of this out yet. Being new to the guy/girl scene, most guys are looking for clues about how this situation works. How you respond to his behavior will give him a good idea of how you want to be treated.

Take This Quick Quiz.

Does he have what it takes? (Check one box per statement)

a. ☐ **Yes** ☐ **No** *He takes initiative to treat you well.* Does he open doors, carry your backpack, or ask your opinion on things? That's class. Be sure to thank him and he'll get the message that you notice and appreciate it!

b. ☐ **Yes** ☐ **No** *He looks for ways to make you comfortable.* Does he show that he's not thinking only of himself? How? Keep your eyes open for signs.

c. ☐ **Yes** ☐ **No** *He adjusts according to your likes and dislikes.* Is he thinking about who you are as a person and showing that he thinks of you as more than a different species? Can he roll with the punches when you tell him what you enjoy?

d. ☐ **Yes** ☐ **No** *He considers your desires and needs before his own.* This may be the hardest one of all to answer since it requires such extraordinary maturity. You may have to wait a while for a guy like this— many grown men don't even have this.

Okay. There are two sides to every coin, so we have to ask: Are *you* acting like the kind of girl who would attract such a Prince Charming? Think about it. Maturity attracts maturity. Class attracts class. Long-lasting relationships are based on you both bringing out the *best* in each other.

If you're looking for certain qualities in a guy, make sure you're also developing the kind of integrity and character that would attract someone like that. If you want to be treated like a true lady, you have to act like one.

Foolproof Test

If you want to know what a guy is really made of, watch him around other women: his mother, sisters, cousins, or friends. You can also tell a lot about a guy by the way he treats his family. If he's rude or sarcastic, you can bet he'll eventually be the same with you. If there's love and respect in those relationships, you've found a winner!

Most of all, remember you don't have to go around trying to "find" a future husband. Someone once said, "Desperation is the world's worst perfume." Being a guy-chaser will not get you the guy you want. Relax and be patient. When the time is right, God will bring "Mr. Right" into your life—if that is His plan for you. In the meantime, have fun making guy friends. Learn how to interact with them. They'll help you discover what guys are like. Enjoy those friendships without all the pressure.

Spend your teen years becoming all God wants you to be. Then someday when you stand at the altar with the man of your dreams you'll be able to say, "Wow! I'm the luckiest girl in the world to have found this incredible man!"

And guess what? He'll be able to say the same about you!

Good Sex– God's Way

Sex is everywhere.

You head to the movies with your girlfriends. Twenty minutes into it, the stars are grabbing at each other's clothes. Five minutes of sweaty groping and you're starting to feel a little more than uncomfortable.

Your best friend shows you a teen magazine on a field trip. It's supposed to be the fashion issue, but the pictures are of models who are hardly wearing anything—and the Q & A column leaves even less to the imagination.

There's no way around it. We live in a sexualized society. Advertisers use sex to sell everything from motorcycles to soap. Musicians sing about it. Even your school might teach you that you can have all the sex you want as long as you use "protection." It's tough to try to stay pure with all the information that's thrown at you, but it's possible. You *can* make it!

God's Ideal

Do you dream about romance and your wedding? Do you think saving sex would make it even better? Do you wonder if God really designed it that way?

No, these aren't trick questions. Your teen years are the time when your body shifts into high gear and you start thinking about romance—and its distant cousin, sex—a lot more frequently.

Maybe you haven't heard much about sex in your church. It can be an awkward topic to talk about, but it's one that every person deals with, Christian and non-Christian.

Why? Because God made us.

God created sex. He chose to make it. It wasn't an afterthought or something bad that entered the world with sin. God looked at Adam after He'd just created him and He said, "He needs a partner." So He created woman and then He told them to "be fruitful and multiply." And how were they supposed to accomplish that? S-E-X. Genesis 1:31: "God saw all that He had made, and it was very good." God saw man and woman and the sex He had designed and He pronounced it not just good—but very good.

Why Sex Turns Ugly

So why is it that people treat sex like it's something forbidden, secret, wrong, or embarrassing? If anything, we should be reveling in it because God made it for us to enjoy, right?

The fact is that sex is about connection, communication, and union on the deepest level humanly possible. Sex is two people joining in a way that makes them physically, mentally, emotionally, and even spiritually *one*. It's more than a physical act. It's the ultimate expression of trust, vulnerability, passion, and commitment. Sex is creation; it is how new life is formed. Sex is the expression of love and the celebration of pleasure. It can be thrilling, deep, and rapturous.

But there's a catch. It only becomes so when it's done right. Otherwise, no matter what you've heard or seen to the contrary, it will become the exact opposite: unsatisfying, deeply painful, and destroying. Ever heard that with great power comes great responsibility? The statement has never been truer than with sex.

You can think of sex like fire. The right use—like a warm campfire or a bright candle—can save your life. The wrong use—like a match to your living room curtains or to pine needles in a forest—kills. God created sex to be good and enjoyable, but He also set up some specific guidelines for sex. He wasn't just trying to take away all the fun. He knew it would be a very powerful gift: one with the power to connect or destroy people on the deepest level. He made it to be a gift that would bind a man and a woman forever—so He made it to only be used within the bond of marriage.

Of course, along with every other good thing he could distort, Satan twisted and perverted sex. There is no one on earth who has not been directly affected by the damage and destruction sex can cause: addictions, diseases, rape, incest, exploitation of every kind, countless lives ruined, and even children dead because of sex and its horrible repercussions. There's plenty to the dark side.

The goal for Christian men and women is to win back the gift by staying absolutely focused on God's plan in order to glorify Him with it. If you desire to please God with your life, and you plan to celebrate your love for God and your husband in marriage, you must commit to waiting for God to unite you to that one man.

Sure, you think. I'd love to do that. But I've got years till I'll be married and how do I know what you're saying is true or not? You don't know what God has planned for me. For all I know, my husband will be old and ugly.

You're right. We don't know what God has planned for your life. But ask yourself if you really want to challenge this. Why be one of the women who thinks nothing bad will happen if you don't decide to wait? Plenty of women and men before you thought they could still glorify God with the rest of their lives and keep their sexuality for themselves. In fact, you probably know some women who did decide that. Maybe you think nothing bad happened to them for deciding what they did.

The truth is that no one can worship God with her whole life while keeping a part back from Him. If you want to have a happy, satisfying life, you have to commit to worshiping Him with your sexuality, as well as the rest of you.

So right now, let Him have control of your sexuality and decide to follow His path of purity while you wait. Romans 12:1 calls it "offer[ing] your bodies as living sacrifices, holy and pleasing to God." It means laying the gift of sex at God's feet and trusting Him to protect it until it's time. And in fact, we really aren't left with any other option. Either we commit to waiting and allowing sex to be the beautiful, fulfilling, exciting thing it was intended to be, or we damage ourselves (and others), weaken the gift, and have to deal with the consequences later.

It may sound harsh, but girl, it's just the plain facts.

Blasting the Myths

The lies about sex are everywhere. Some are easy to recognize. Others are sneaky and subtle. Have you recognized any of these media messages lately?

"Everybody's doing it."

"Flaunting your sexuality means you're a real woman."

"If you want to prove it to him, have sex with him."

"Trying to control it is foolish; just do it."

"Your body was made to be enjoyed; why deny it?"

"Sex is like any other sport: The idea is to score as much as you can."

"You can always just go back to the way it was before."

"If you know you're ready, then everything's fine."

"A condom is all you need to protect you."

"All teens have sex; it's stupid to think you can stop them."

"Men will be disappointed if you don't say yes."

"If you get a guy worked up, it's your responsibility to follow through."

"Sex always brings deeper relationships and romance."

"You're supposed to have sex when you're young; that's like the point."

"Virginity is a joke; mature women have sex."

"Live for today; who knows when you'll get another chance?"

What God Says

"Love is eternal; it waits forever."

"Love wants what's best for the other."

"Passion is strong; My passion for you is the strongest you will ever know."

"I made sex for you to enjoy in marriage."

"Sex will always leave an impression, either beautiful or horrible."

"Nobody can 'just do it' and get out unscathed."

"Beauty means respecting your body, realizing that it is My holy temple."

"Sex is not something your timetable or your feelings can determine."

"Nothing but My plan can protect you from the damage sex causes."

"I made you able to decide because it is your decision."

"No one has a right to your body but Me."

"Sex follows commitment and trust. It never brings romance."

"Innocence is fragile; once it is broken, it can't come back."

"Any animal can have sex. Few people will know the way I designed it to be."

Some Passages Pertaining to Sex

Genesis 2:21-25	Job 31:1
Proverbs 5	Proverbs 6:27-29
Proverbs 7	Song of Solomon 2:7
Matthew 5:27-30	1 Corinthians 6:12-20
1 Corinthians 7:1-11	Galatians 5:19
Ephesians 5:3	Colossians 3:1-10
1 Thessalonians 4:3-7	Titus 2:12-13
Hebrews 13:4	Revelation 21:8

Living Beyond the Moment

With every year of life, we embark on new adventures. We experience our first steps, our first words, and our first day of school. Maybe you were a Girl Scout, took gymnastics, and got the chicken pox in first grade.

As you think back through the years, you can come up with a long list of experiences that were new and probably difficult at the time. Maybe your first day of school was scary; maybe going camping in the woods with your troop was terrifying; doing your gymnastics routine for the class's parents may have been the worst of all.

But by now, you're on the other side of these experiences. You know that difficult moments pass, time moves on, and the thrill of having lived through those things successfully is a reason to feel pride.

Now, you're entering a new phase. Today, you stand on the brink of teendom. The next adventure is here. What new things will you experience and accomplish? Which ones will be unique to you, and which will be familiar to all teen girls around the globe?

Every teen girl, in every walk of life, undergoes enormous changes in her feelings. She'll no longer think boys are disgusting—at least not *all* of them. She'll actually feel *attracted* to some of them and once she gets to know them better, she will develop deeper feelings that can bring back that earlier terror.

So what's a girl to do?

Part of the Plan

Strong feelings are common for girls at all ages. The strong attraction to and desire for men is built right into the female makeup. You can experience strong feelings just thinking about a cute guy. You'll definitely experience them when a relationship with him begins to develop.

The warmth and exhilaration of all that emotion is just the beginning of God's plan for sexual intimacy. You want to hold his hand, kiss him, touch him. And though this new adventure is all part of the design for women, there will be times when the feelings become difficult to control or understand.

The Difficulty

Those new feelings that all teen girls experience are meant to be acted on—within a special context. That context, of course, is the commitment of marriage. And most teen girls are nowhere near getting married. So what do you do with all the excitement you're already feeling?

This is where the difficulty comes into the adventure. You made it through difficult moments in the past, but nothing like this. How do you know you'll be able to do it again?

The best way to deal with your feelings in a way that honors God is to develop a specific plan of action. If you move through the adventure without one, you're likely to lose your way and wander around making huge, potentially disastrous mistakes. But luckily, you're starting out right. You can set a goal and design a plan to get you to your goal. That's half the battle right there. You're already much more likely to avoid the typical heartache and disappointment that many teen girls face.

The next step is to start asking the right questions . . .

How Far Is Too Far?

One of the most frequently asked questions we get is the ol' "How far can I go in a physical relationship?" We're tempted to say something really corny like, "About a block, then head straight home," but we know you won't laugh. So let's get real serious real fast, okay?

You have a responsibility as a Christian young lady.

Wait a sec. Are you going to get into all that stuff about responsibilities? I thought we were talking about sex.

Point taken. We can talk about sex, but with sex, it's necessary to talk about responsibility. So stick with us, and we'll go straight for the facts.

Fact #1

Your job right now (and in life forever) is to get as close to Jesus Christ as possible.

You may consider school to be your main job right now. But your biggest job, your top priority, your purpose in life isn't to earn good grades, find the perfect guy, or figure out what career you want to pursue. You main job is to love Jesus and strengthen your relationship with Him. So instead of pouring your thoughts and energy into asking *How far can I go with my boyfriend and still be okay?* start to pour that energy into deepening your most important relationship.

Fact #2

However far you choose to go, you'll have to tell your future husband about it someday.

Chances are, you're not currently dating the guy you'll end up marrying. Would you like to find out he was messing around as much as possible before he met you? The same thing applies to you. Pray that you'll be able to respect that man you'll eventually know completely. And while you're at it, you might want to pray that God will keep him pure for a lifetime of marriage with *you*.

And you know what? Your future husband may be praying for you right now too.

Fact #3

The idea behind the honeymoon isn't for two professional lovers to have a polished performance!

A honeymoon isn't supposed to be where you can show off all your sexual experience! It's just the beginning of all the great experiences to come. The honeymoon is where two people first open God's wonderful gift together. Any previous experience just ruins the surprise.

Take This Quick Quiz.

What is the purpose of dating? (Check all that you think apply.)

☐ **a.** To become a good kisser.

☐ **b.** To learn how to carry on a conversation with the opposite sex without throwing up.

☐ **c.** To discover what qualities in a guy are important for a long-term relationship.

☐ **d.** To learn about sex.

☐ **e.** To develop social skills.

☐ **f.** To become better friends with the opposite sex.

If you checked **a** or **d**, you have reason to be worried. Those are not reasons to date. If, however, you checked the other answers, you're on target! You're aware that your dating years are not to be used practicing for your future honeymoon—rather, your honeymoon and everything leading up to it— is to be saved for a lifetime of marriage.

Fact #4 — God desires for you to live a life of sexual purity.

Since God invented sex, He obviously knows how, when, and where it works best. And He's made it crystal clear that sex outside of marriage is sin.

Maybe you've already made a commitment to save sex until you're married. Terrific! If you haven't, we hope you'll do that by the end of this chapter. But first, maybe we should chat about what sexual purity is and isn't.

A lot of teens mistakenly think, *As long as I don't have sexual intercourse until I'm married, I'm fine. I'm still a virgin.*

Sexual purity and virginity are not the same things.

Anyone can say NO to intercourse. But when God commands us not to have sex until marriage, He's talking about sexual *intimacy*—not simply refraining from the act of intercourse.

Take This Quick Quiz.

What *is* sexual intimacy? (Check all that apply.)

- ☐ **a.** Holding hands.
- ☐ **b.** Lying under the covers together.
- ☐ **c.** Watching TV together.
- ☐ **d.** Kissing on the cheek.
- ☐ **e.** Walking arm in arm.
- ☐ **f.** French-kissing.
- ☐ **g.** Undressing each other.

Actually, *all* of these are potentially intimate. Each one can act like glue in a relationship. When you hold hands with a guy, you feel more comfortable. Chances are, next time you'll do it again. Or go further.

Of course there's nothing wrong with holding hands. But because it's a physical act between a guy and a girl, it's potentially a bonding agent drawing you closer together. And the more you're physically involved, the more glued together you naturally become.

God does not say no to sex outside of marriage to kill the fun. It's actually to make it more fun later and to protect you now. He designed sex to be the ultimate glue possible. That's why it's so hard to try to stop it from sticking you to a guy. The problem with holding hands or making out is that you're trying to get glue not to stick.

Sex in its ideal form is designed to start and go, *go,* GO until you reach the finish line. Your choices are either being frustrated trying to keep the glue from sticking, or to follow God's plan by sticking to His design.

Fact #5 — Your kisses are extremely valuable.

Think about it: Each time you kiss a guy, you give part of yourself away. And again, it's not necessarily wrong, but it does make things more difficult later on. Your kisses are extremely valuable, not just to others but to you. That's why it's so important to be selective about whom you choose to kiss. Let God help you with that decision. He cares more about your kisses than even you do!

Kissing just to try it, or because it feels good, or because you had a great time with a guy and feel as though you *owe him* something are terrible reasons to give away a kiss. Way too many teens are giving their kisses away too freely. Again, be selective. Don't kiss without an extremely good reason.

Fact #6 — Set your standards now.

Have you taken time to set dating standards for yourself? If not, right now would be a great time to do it! There are simply too many options and risks in waiting until you're in a relationship before you think about these things. Seek God's guidance as you do this. I'll list several statements, and you mark where you think you should be with that standard (you may want to ask your mom, youth pastor, or counselor for input and discussion on these).

Take This Quick Quiz.

Agree	Unsure	Disagree	(Check one box per statement.)
☐	☐	☐	**a.** I'll only date Christian guys.
☐	☐	☐	**b.** I'll only date Christian guys who share my theology.
☐	☐	☐	**c.** I'll never allow myself to be alone with a guy where no adults are present.
☐	☐	☐	**d.** I won't kiss a guy unless I am in a committed relationship with him.
☐	☐	☐	**e.** I won't kiss until I'm engaged.
☐	☐	☐	**f.** I won't kiss until my wedding.
☐	☐	☐	**g.** I won't let a guy touch me below the neck.
☐	☐	☐	**h.** I won't touch a guy below his neck.
☐	☐	☐	**i.** It's okay to go camping alone with a guy and share the same tent.
☐	☐	☐	**j.** It's okay to share the same sleeping bag with my boyfriend.
☐	☐	☐	**k.** I'll hold hands with every guy I go out with.
☐	☐	☐	**l.** If I'm engaged, I'll be free to become more sexually involved.

Fact #7 God forgives.

Maybe you've already been sexually involved. Perhaps you haven't had intercourse, but you've been sexually intimate. Guess what! God wants to forgive you and wipe your slate clean. The exciting thing about Christianity is that God forgives and completely forgets!

True repentance isn't, *Okay, I'll ask God to forgive me now. But tomorrow night I'll go ahead and give in to Jeremy, because I know I can ask God to forgive me again tomorrow night.*

Although God forgives a repentant heart, that's not a repentant attitude. True repentance is, *Oh, Father! I am so sorry. I have wronged You and sinned against You by breaking Your commands. Will You forgive me? I don't ever plan on going down that road again!*

See the difference?

If you've already blown it and you want to start over, God would love to make you a "spiritual virgin." You can pray about it right now:

Dear Jesus:

I've blown it sexually. I've gone too far. I have sinned, and I'm so sorry. I'd love to be forgiven and start over. Will You forgive me, Jesus? I commit right now to abstain from sexual intimacy until marriage. I realize I can't keep this promise in my own strength. I need Your help. Please empower me with Your Holy Spirit and enable me to keep this pledge. And Jesus, help me not to place myself in tempting situations where I would be more prone to break this precious commitment.

Amen.

Fact #8

Your job is to get as close to Jesus Christ as possible.

(Yeah, that's a repeat of Fact #1, but it's so important we gotta say it again!)

See, the real issue isn't, "How far can I go and still live a holy life?" The real issue is, "God, what can I do to deepen my relationship with You? I don't want to settle for 'Casual Christian'; I want to live a life of obedience to You."

When you're asking the second question, the first suddenly isn't that important. Why? Because you're not trying to please a guy . . . and you're not trying to please yourself— you're pleasing your Lord and Savior.

If you've never made a commitment to sexual purity, you can do that right now!

Pray this pledge, and sign your name at the bottom.

I believe that God designed sexual intimacy for marriage and marriage only. Therefore, I promise not to steal from my future husband by being sexually intimate outside of marriage. I want God's very best for my life. I pledge, with God's help, to maintain my sexual purity until marriage.

Name ————————————————— Date ————

Check Out These Books on Sex and Purity!

- *What Hollywood Won't Tell You About Sex, Love and Dating*
  —by Greg Johnson and Susie Shellenberger

- *Anybody Got a Clue About Guys?*
  —by Susie Shellenberger

- *And the Bride Wore White*
  —by Dannah Gresh

- *I Kissed Dating Goodbye*
  —by Joshua Harris

Setting (and Meeting) Your Goal

So, first thing you want to look at is what your hope is in living with your sexual feelings. For example, do you hope to be a girl who exposes her feelings to every guy who shows interest? Do you hope to live recklessly and just see how far you can get before your sexual feelings lead you into trouble? Or do you hope to see what it is those sexual feelings are leading you to, on the other side of marriage?

Christian women who want to live in obedience to God's will, work to match their lifestyles with God's design. The following verses are a great goal to set in handling your sexual feelings.

"It is God's will that you should be sanctified: that you should avoid sexual immorality; that each of you should learn to control his own body in a way that is holy and honorable, not in passionate lust like the heathen, who do not know God" (1 Thessalonians 4:3-5).

In thinking and praying about your goal, imagine yourself as an adult, where you want to be, and how you hope to feel. Talk with your parents and other trusted adults and discuss what boundaries they set at your age for their sexual feelings. If you do all that, you will have plenty of information for setting the goal you need to make it through this new territory.

Practical How-To's

Let's say living a life that pleases God and protects your heart, soul, body, and mind is your goal. Great. But now you've got to think about how you're going to reach it.

Try some of these things and you'll be well on your way.

1   Scripture

It's easy to become distracted from your goal and find yourself thinking or doing things that move you away from God. To avoid this, you need to remind yourself of your goal often. Verses that encourage you to follow the path of sexual purity can help.

Memorizing some of them would be even better. Here are a few to get you started: Job 27:5-6, 1 Corinthians 6:18-20, Ephesians 5:3, and Titus 2:11-14.

2   Prayer

Thoughts and feelings contrary to God's aren't something you need to tackle on your own. Oh, you can try, but don't expect to make it very far. To reach your goal of living beyond the moment, ask God for His help. As your creator and Father, He knows every detail of your feelings. Run to Him when your feelings bombard you, and ask Him for strength to handle them wisely.

3 Honesty and Accountability

While it's terrific to be honest with God about your feelings and to rely on His strength to get you through difficult moments, it's also helpful to turn to a parent, a trusted adult, or a mature friend. Be honest with someone else about the feelings you're experiencing. Share your goal, and ask this person to keep you accountable in meeting it. This means asking you some tough questions you'll have to be honest about. She should ask what your mind has been focusing on and whether how you dealt with it moved you toward or away from your goal.

4 Wise Actions

When it's all said and done, reaching your goal comes down to what you decide to do with your feelings. No one else can live your life for you. You are responsible for your decisions and actions. Through Bible study, prayer, and accountability, you can set yourself on the course of living beyond destructive thoughts and the common moments of weakness.

It will be difficult, but remember: Your struggles will pass, time will move on, and the thrill of having made it through successfully will be reason to shout, "Yes! I did it!"

One day, God will give you even bigger adventures; adventures that you can explore to your heart's content. Waiting for it might seem uncool, weird, or foolish to some, but the challenge proves it's much more than that. Just imagine all the regrets you'll never have because of the time you spent living beyond the moment!

Part Three At Home and School

Why Parents Sometimes Bug You

What is it that usually makes those parents of yours crank you up? Probably most of the everyday problems you run into fall into one of these five categories:

- **Control Issues**
- **Safety Issues**
- **Trust Issues**
- **Differing Expectations**
- **Relational Issues**

Control Issues basically boil down to "Who's in charge here?" The answer (for as long as you're living in their house) is Mom and Dad. You'll gain more independence as you show maturity and responsibility, but it's always in your best interest to remember that for better or worse, the owner of the house you live in is the one who gets to set the rules.

When it comes to the **Safety Issues,** overprotective parents can really be a bummer. From the twentieth time they warned you not to touch the hot stove, to the lecture about the dangers of underage drinking, you've been guarded, safe, protected, and hopefully unhurt. Parents can't protect you from everything and of course worrying about you sort of comes with the job. It's part of parents' DNA—when you're out riding in a car with a boy or some friends, parents will feel anxious. What are you gonna do?

Here are a few things:

- Let them know where you're going.

- Let them know if plans change.

- Let them know you're making wise choices about your activities.

- Let them get to know your friends or boyfriend.

Actually, that's really just one big thing, isn't it? *Let them know. Communicate.* Ultimately, it's going to be better to show them you understand their concern. Once they see that you get it, they may start to ease up a bit. And besides, would you rather have parents who don't love you and never worry what happens to you?

Sometimes a parent's worry about your safety can make it seem he or she doesn't trust you. Other times, you've done something to break that trust and it seems as though that single failure affects every decision they make about you. With **Trust Issues**, there are many things that can damage or sever completely the thin strand of trust between teens and their parents. We'll talk more about this issue later.

Another common gripe is when parents try to live the lives they missed out on through their children. This is a case of **Differing Expectations**: parents expecting their kids to be just like them and enjoy the same things they did. Maybe your mom was homecoming queen and now expects you to "continue the legacy." How in the world are you supposed to deal with that?

First of all, be honest. If you don't have any interest in being the debutante in the princess parade, you don't have to feel guilty or endure a miserable experience just to meet your mom's expectation. Maybe you want to pursue your talent in art or soccer instead.

At the same time, it may be your expectations that need adjusting. If you just don't like doing homework, your parents have the right to expect you to give your best effort, whether or not you feel like it.

For the early part of your life, your **Relationship** with your parents had a huge influence over you—what you did, how you dressed, what you believed. As you enter the teen years, that influence naturally lessens as you develop more independence. Whether you (or your parents) like it or not, you will begin paying more attention to other influences—your friends, your teachers, music, movies, etc.—than your parents.

So how do you keep these other things from derailing your relationship with Mom and Dad?

One way is to let the "opposing forces" meet. If Mom and Dad can see the people you're hanging out with, chances are they will feel more comfortable in loosening up the reins.

Now let's talk about a few ways to take care of some of these issues constructively.

It's a Jungle in Here!

Ever seen an old rerun of *Leave It to Beaver*? In that famous TV show from the 1950s, June Cleaver would meet her husband at the door wearing a neatly pressed dress, perfect makeup, always smiling and offering information on what she's spent all afternoon cooking for dinner.

Life has obviously changed since the '50s and the average American family no longer recognizes the Cleavers as normal. Both Mom and Dad work and come home exhausted. That means frozen dinners or pizza if you're lucky. Every night someone's on the run to practice, sports events, meetings, Bible study, part-time jobs, youth group, friends' houses, social events. Meals together as a family are pretty rare. Communication gets forgotten, schedules get mixed up, responsibilities get missed. It's easy to get frustrated with each other when you're so busy. The frenetic pace only adds to the conflict that naturally exists when you mix in hormone swings, siblings, and exhausted parents.

Little things become big things when you're stretched too thin. Why is Dad in such a bad mood? If you knew he'd lost that big account, you'd have known it wasn't the best time to ask for that pair of jeans you want. Then maybe you'd know what "the big deal" was and that just because everybody at school is wearing them doesn't mean he doesn't understand.

Jealousy, selfishness—even little inconsiderations—can start a fight from the tiniest things. If conflict can't be avoided, how do we cope with it? Nobody likes the whole family to be in a bad mood, yet we all have our little "things" that push our buttons and first thing you know, voices are raised, doors are slamming, and feelings are hurt. Sometimes even the dog runs for cover. *Why can't we be a normal family?*

What's Normal?

Like it or not, you are a normal family. Conflict is part of every family, even loving and close ones. Any time you have two or more people involved in something, you have different personalities, different opinions, and different ideas about what's priority. Your family members are those you're most comfortable around, and home is where you let down when you're tired or frustrated. Multiply that by Mom, Dad, brothers and sisters, and there's a good chance frayed nerves are going to get on each other's frayed nerves. The end result? Conflict.

Take heart. You're not alone. There will always be the normal parent/teen conflict causing issues over the music you listen to, the clothes you wear, the color of hair you want, or how many holes you'd like in your ears. Curfews, friends, allowances, what movies you watch . . . there are a multitude of potential disagreements you'll have with Mom or Dad during your teen years. It can't be avoided, but conflict can be greatly reduced at your house if you follow a few basic guidelines.

The Golden Rule

Remember the "Golden Rule"? We all learned it in the first grade: "Treat others the way you want to be treated." Know what? That even applies to your family! Taking the time to be sensitive to each other's schedules, frustrations, and likes and dislikes is a good start to eliminating some of the conflict at home.

Read between the lines. Understand that Mom and Dad have pressures way bigger than they may let on to. So choose the best time to approach them with a request or a not-so-good report card. Thoughtfulness and consideration play a key role in family relationships. How's your ability to read between the lines? Let's find out!

Take This Quick Quiz.

It's all in the timing. (Check one box per statement.)

a. Dad stubs his toe coming in from the backyard. You tell him about the dent you put in the car this morning.

☐ great timing ☐ lousy timing

b. Dad soaks his foot, eats dinner, and has read the paper. You tell him about the dent you put in the car this morning.

☐ great timing ☐ lousy timing

c. Your brother gets a $50 speeding ticket, and he just lost his part-time job. You decide to remind him he never paid you back the $20 he owes you.

☐ great timing ☐ lousy timing

d. You hear about your brother's ticket and decide to write him a note saying you can do without the $20 he owes you until after he finds another job.

☐ great timing ☐ lousy timing

87

Be honest. Tell your parents the truth and the *whole* truth. The first time. Leaving out important details can make all the difference in whether you have to deal with an issue only once or again later on as new details emerge. You can count on this: Your parents will usually find out somehow. It might as well be from you first.

Respect your parents' authority. They're the parents; you're the kid. They're responsible for you physically, financially, and spiritually. If they still say "no" after you've calmly discussed it and shared your point of view, no matter how much you disagree, it's your responsibility to accept their decision as the God-given authority figures in your life. Someday, when you're the parent, you'll understand this completely.

What's in It for You

God doesn't always expect you to agree with your folks. He knows they'll make mistakes. But He does expect you to honor them with your obedience. And for those who do? He gives a fantastic promise. Check it out: "Children, obey your parents in the Lord, for this is right. 'Honor your father and mother'— which is the first commandment with a promise—'that it may go well with you and that you may enjoy long life on the earth'" (Ephesians 6:1-3).

Want a long life full of blessing? Honor your parents. And when conflict does arise, ask God to help you through it. He will!

The 10 "T's" of Talking

Maybe you aren't in the midst of a major battle, but there's something you want to get across. To ensure you'll be heard, your best shot is with these 10 "T's" of talking.

1. **Think** about what you're going to say ahead of time. Plan the points of what you're suggesting and anticipate answers to any objections they may have.

2. **Target** your goal and see if there are any points you can negotiate.

3. **Temper** literally means "to moderate or control." Make sure yours is under control no matter what happens. If you lose it, you lose your point, too.

4. **Timing** is everything. When Dad first walks in the door from work or while Mom is getting little brother ready for bed are not good times to talk.

5. **Thoughtfulness** goes a long way in getting your arguments across.

6. **Two-way** conversation is the name of the game.

7. **Telling** is not yelling. Even if you're getting frustrated, you can make sure it remains a conversation instead of a shouting match.

8. **Teamwork.** Engaging each other as teammates shows that you want to work together to get the issue resolved. For example, if it's going out Saturday night, ask your parents to trust that you'll be bright-eyed for church in the morning.

9. **Tone** of voice and your inflection is vital for healthy discussion. If you sound demanding or disrespectful, get ready to tell your friends the plans are off.

10. **Thank** God once the conversation is done, regardless of the outcome. Show your appreciation to your teammates for helping you learn to communicate well.

Any home has its times of turbulence. But once you're past them, your family will still be your family. And from that perspective, the wins and losses don't look so important.

Keys to Responsibility

"You're so unfair! You don't even trust me!"

"All of my friends already get to!"

"I never get to decide for myself!"

Any of these sound familiar?

Phrases like these are common ammunition in a teen's fight for independence. But the question is if your parents were teens once too, why don't they get it?

Wouldn't it be great if there was a way to get your parents to finally get it? How can you get them to trust you more and give you freedom to make your own decisions? Keep reading!

1 Ease into it

It's hard to believe, but your becoming a teenager snuck up on your parents. Yeah, they knew it was coming, but they really weren't prepared for the day it became official.

Know what else? It scared them to death.

But how could they possibly be surprised? you ask. *They had 13 years to prepare for it!*

We know; it's weird. But somehow those 13 years slipped right by before they noticed.

Well, that's not my fault! you say.

You're right. It's not. But give 'em a break. They need a little time to adjust to the whole idea of you becoming more independent and making more of your own decisions. It scares them, not because they don't think you're a great kid, or worry that you can't be trusted, but because giving you more freedom means they won't always be there should anything happen or if you need their help.

Of course, that's the whole point. You don't want them to always be there helping and giving advice. But hey . . . from Mom and Dad's point of view, there's a big scary world out there! You really can't blame them for wanting to protect you, can you? That's their job. The key is to ease them into making your own choices and being independent without them worrying every time you leave the house without them.

Okay, so how do I do that? Glad you asked.

2 Be trustworthy

Trust is something that has to be earned. You can't expect your parents to hand over the car keys the minute you turn 16 and say, "Okay, Honey, go for it!" They have to know you're prepared and can handle the responsibility. You go through driver's training and hours of behind-the-wheel practice with your parents or an instructor, right? Driving takes a lot of practice. You work up to it for months before you're out with the car alone. Your parents watch your progress and gain a comfort level with your ability to maneuver and drive safely.

It's the same with becoming more independent. Your parents want to be assured you're making wise choices. All teens are going to make some wrong choices; that's part of the learning process. We all learn by our experiences and the consequences that come with our mistakes. Yet the more you show your parents you can be trusted to do what you say you're going to do, and be where you say you're going to be, the more freedom they're likely to give you. If you have a curfew, stick to their rules and be home on time. If they ask you to call if you're going to be late, CALL! Being considerate of their wishes shows that you're responsible. It demonstrates your respect.

But their rules are so unreasonable! you say. *My other friends don't even have a curfew!* Arguing and fussing at your parents is not likely to get you more freedom. In fact, it'll probably backfire on you. As you show maturity and obedience to their rules, they'll see that you can be trusted, and over time, those rules may change a bit.

On the other hand, if you sneak out of the house and lie about where you're going, they're not going to trust you even when you do tell the truth. Be smart. Honest and frequent communication with your parents will help them trust you, which will make them loosen the reins a little. They *want* to trust you. So show them they can.

There's actually a place in the Bible that talks about this. Ever heard the parable about a man who gave his employees some things to take care of while he was gone? Two of them invested and earned more money. Another just buried it in the ground. The moral of the story (or one of them, anyway) is if you want to be given greater responsibilities, you have to prove you know how to handle the ones you're given.

RESPONSIBLE

3 Work to your own advantage

Your parents are looking for signs that you're not an irresponsible, argumentative adolescent. You can gain so much trust and respect by simply communicating with them instead of whining. If you disagree with a rule or a decision, try asking them if you can talk about it instead of getting mad and storming out of the room.

Here are two different approaches to a conflict. Which one do you think might get Mom or Dad to reconsider your viewpoint?

1. "Mo-om! What do you mean I can't hike across Afghanistan? You guys are soooo unfair! I hate your rules! I wish I could move to Antarctica. I hate your cooking and I hate that stupid blouse!"

2. "I understand your concern about the Middle East and all, but I really want to make this trip. Can we sit down together and make a list of pros and cons and discuss it? Then if you still don't like it, you can make the final decision."

Disagreements are going to happen. Count on it. So wait until everyone's calmed down and has had a chance to think. By gently asking them to reconsider the situation and your point of view, they may be willing to think about it and compromise. That way you'll at least have half a chance they'll change their mind. They just may have been caught off guard and need a few minutes to think about it. Angry words and tantrums only close the door to further conversation.

And if they still won't budge, respect and obey them. They're your protectors and they have your safety and well-being in mind. If they do reconsider, thank them, and do your best to show you respect their decision. With any luck, they'll see your maturity and take that into consideration the next time.

If you're considerate of their concerns and polite in your conversations, your respect will prove you use good judgment even when you don't agree with them. A rebellious spirit will get you nowhere. Often parents try to spare their children the same pain and mistakes they made as a teen, and in doing so, they may seem overprotective. Try to understand that their love for you may sometimes seem like anything but love. Something that may seem harmless may actually have long-term consequences if your parents allowed it. Sometimes parents foresee danger where you can't see it. They may know something you don't about a certain person, place, or activity that could be disastrous for you.

4 Take the initiative

Be assertive in showing your parents that you're becoming more responsible. Clean your room before they nag you for a week. Go ahead and empty the dishwasher. Wash the car without being asked. Do your own laundry. The more you show your parents you're willing to handle, the sooner they'll be willing to give you freedom. You can help the process along by your cooperative attitude and willingness to prove yourself able to make good decisions and accept the consequences when mistakes happen. Make them proud of you!

Seven Rules for Fighting Fair

1. Stick to the point. If you really want to solve the disagreement, don't bring up unrelated issues.

2. Don't get personal. Snotty remarks can hurt long after the issue has been settled.

3. Provide time to cool off. If you're getting upset, leave for a while to think about alternatives instead of just pulling out the heavy artillery.

4. Figure out the problem. Is it a question of personal preference (like music) or of right and wrong (you broke curfew and didn't call)?

5. Realize what you hope to gain. You don't want to "win" the argument and end up damaging the relationship.

6. Decide when to walk away. You're not giving up; you just realize that some beaches are not worth dying on.

7. Don't hold a grudge. Resentment can pop up when you least expect it.

You have more control over how much freedom your parents give you than you probably realize. If you do everything listed here, your parents will soon realize that you can make good decisions. You can choose whether to be compliant and agreeable, or argumentative and miserable. Your attitude during this period of change and adjustment can make all the difference.

Do your part to minimize conflict and misunderstanding with your parents, and your teen years can be some of the best times your family has together. Let them know your schedule and what's going on in your life. Fill them in on your weekend plans, outings with friends, sporting events, and your work schedule so there are no surprises or double-bookings. That way, they'll know you can be trusted and they'll have confidence in your ability to manage your own life.

How to Earn Back Your Parents' Trust

T. *Truth*—Acknowledge that you made a mistake.

R. *Responsibility*—Make it right by promising to try to avoid future bad decisions.

U. *Understanding*—Recognize your parents' disappointment.

S. *Submission*—Accept your parents' authority in the situation.

T. *Time*—Wait for them to be convinced they won't be disappointed again.

Surviving Divorce

Know that oldies song: "They say that breaking up is hard to do"? It may be a bit of an understatement, but without a doubt, when families break up, it's a hard thing.

If you've endured a divorce, separation, or severe family tension, you know the pain. With marriages falling apart in more and more households, you're not alone. But even so, how do you make your way through? Who do you turn to?

Keep reading. With God's help, you *can* get through this.

Tip #1 — Turn to God for comfort and help.

Jesus understands your emotion better than you do. Only He knows your every thought. Spend time in prayer and reading the Bible. Allow yourself to grieve before God. Ask Him your tough questions. Recovering from a major loss can sometimes take many years, so make a commitment to the long haul of healing.

"He who dwells in the shelter of the Most High will rest in the shadow of the Almighty. I will say of the LORD, 'He is my refuge and my fortress, my God, in whom I trust' " (Psalm 91:1-2).

Tip #2 — Your parents' relationship is not your fault.

Maybe you got involved in some arguments sometimes or yelled or made things difficult. You may feel you were the source of an argument between your parents or maybe your parents actually blamed you directly for their difficulties.

But no matter what a parent says, his or her marriage problems are not your fault. It's just not true. Only your parents are responsible for the decisions they make. You could have contributed to the tension (and if so, you may feel guilty), but you are incapable of being the reason for your parents' problems. Simply, you are a product of their marriage and not the other way around.

If you've been burdened with the idea that your parents' problems are your fault: "Cast your cares on the LORD and he will sustain you; he will never let the righteous fall" (Psalm 55:22).

Tip #3 — Seek help from a trusted adult.

A professional counselor, pastor, teacher, or family friend can help you work through the pain of your parents' divorce or separation. But choose with care. Be sure your parents wouldn't mind if you're sharing the ins and outs of your family life with an outsider. On the other hand, it's difficult for someone to help if he or she doesn't know what you've been through. If you don't get permission from your parents to share the details, it's probably best to share only what you're thinking or feeling as a result. It may be tough to put all of your feelings into spoken words, so writing in a journal, creating poetry, or drawing may help.

HELP

Tip #4 Choose to forgive.

"Therefore, as God's chosen people . . . bear with each other and forgive whatever grievances you may have against one another. Forgive as the Lord forgave you" (Colossians 3:12-13). It's never easy to do, but to move forward, you've got to forgive. How have your parents hurt you? They may not ask for forgiveness, but to be free of it, you'll have to forgive them anyway.

Why? Why forgive someone who isn't even sorry? First, God says we must. Second, He's forgiven you countless times. Third, forgiving helps you let go of anger and bitterness. And you don't need those hanging around.

Sometimes forgiveness is a process. Again, finding a mature friend or counselor who can talk through the issues of forgiveness and pray with you is critical.

Tip #5 — Accept your disappointment.

As much as you may want your parents to reunite, or as much as you dream of them getting along, realize these things are not in your control (in the same way their breaking up wasn't in your control).

But just because life may not work out in the way you want doesn't mean you need to give up hope altogether. Keep praying for your parents and your family. Share your heart's desires with God. Let go of your expectations and you'll be free to look forward to what's to come. "May the God of hope fill you with all joy and peace as you trust in him, so that you may overflow with hope by the power of the Holy Spirit" (Romans 15:13).

Tip #6 — Learn to love and release anger.

God wants us to love as He loves. It may seem impossible, but the Holy Spirit makes you able to love everyone. Ask God to help you *really* love your parents. This means you may need to change the way you talk to them, the way you act around them or the things you do for them.

Now, it's not wrong to be angry. What you need to watch out for is holding on to anger. If you remain angry with your parents, you're holding a grudge, becoming bitter, and doing the exact opposite of loving them. So go ahead and be angry but let it go before it crushes you. If letting go of anger is difficult, turn to God and a trusted adult for help. "'In your anger do not sin': Do not let the sun go down while you are still angry, and do not give the devil a foothold" (Ephesians 4:26-27).

Tip #7 Help your siblings.

You may not always get along with your brothers and sisters, but in divorce, you might be the only source of help to them. As you are strengthened by God, you can share His love with others. As you forgive and let go of anger, you can help siblings who are struggling with the same issues. "Praise be to the God and Father of our Lord Jesus Christ, the Father of compassion and the God of all comfort, who comforts us in all our troubles, so that we can comfort those in any trouble with the comfort we ourselves have received from God" (2 Corinthians 1:3-4).

Tip#8 — Continue your relationship with your parents.

You may not want to see or talk with your parents for a while. That's completely normal. But it's important to maintain communication with them on some level. Give yourself time, and again, ask for help from God and a trusted adult. When relationships are broken they take time to heal. But with God's help, restoration is possible! "Make sure that nobody pays back wrong for wrong, but always try to be kind to each other and to everyone else" (1 Thessalonians 5:15).

Tip#9 — Stay who you are.

While your responsibilities in your household may need to change due to a shift in family members, you need to be able to remain a teen and not turn into an adult overnight. Talk to your parents about this and be careful not to take too much on your shoulders alone.

Tip #10 — Look for good things to come from the bad.

As a child of the Land of Broken Families, you have a future that's in the hands of a loving God. This may not always *feel* true, but you can *know* it's true because of His promise: " 'For I know the plans I have for you,' declares the LORD, 'plans to prosper you and not to harm you, plans to give you hope and a future. Then you will call upon me and come and pray to me, and I will listen to you. You will seek me and find me when you seek me with all your heart' " (Jeremiah 29:11-13).

And remember, you will now be more sensitive to others dealing with divorce. Your difficulties enable you to minister to hurting friends. Your family's situation creates new maturity within you. The process of pain causes growth in many ways.

Finally, coming from a "broken home" motivates you to have a better marriage and family when you marry. God can use these circumstances to teach you in His time and in His ways. "And we know that in all things God works for the good of those who love him, who have been called according to his purpose" (Romans 8:28).

How to Make Friends

Jamie always had a crowd around her. She wasn't beautiful. She had zits and wasn't exceptionally good at sports. But she was someone everyone at school loved. Wherever she went, someone wanted to be with her. It wasn't unusual for Jamie to be seen listening to one of the football players share a problem with her, or to see her showing a new student how to get to the biology lab.

Why? What was it about Jamie that made everyone notice her? If her looks and her talents weren't anything to brag about, what did she have going for her?

Here it is—short and simple—Jamie had learned the secret of making friends.

As you read on, keep in mind that you can't always be popular just by doing and saying nice things. But you can always be making friends. Later, we'll talk about cliques and the ridiculousness of the cool/uncool game. But remember that popularity was never Jesus' goal. He simply loved people—including the freaks and weirdos—and His "popularity" still soared.

The Secret

Jamie's secret to having lots of friends really isn't rocket science. It's pretty basic:

Be nice to everyone!

Wait a sec, you're thinking. *That's too easy. There's gotta be more to making friends than that!*

Okay, yeah. There are five main strategies we're going to talk about, but the biggest secret of all—the one thousands of teens tend to skip over—is simply being nice to people.

Jamie was as kind to the new kids as she was the football player. She had friends in the band and friends in drama. She refused to associate with only one group of people. Because she was kind to everyone, people wanted to be around her.

Here's the Rest

The other strategies for making friends (after being nice to everyone) are:

A sensational smile.

There's something intriguing about someone who smiles a lot. We're automatically drawn to someone who's happy. If people know you're approachable, they'll start coming to you. A smile is an open invitation. It says, "I'm friendly. I'm not going to hurt you."

Learn how to talk and listen.

We all know the girl who talks all the time. She's not much fun to be around, is she? I once had a friend whom I went out with a lot. She talked all the time. As in "nonstop." Once in a while, she'd say, "Susie, I don't understand you. You speak to thousands of teenagers every year, but you sure don't say much one-on-one."

I always wanted to say, "You're just now noticing that?" But even if I had, she would have been off on something else too quickly to notice.

We all want to express ourselves. We all have stories to tell. Yet each of us enjoys having someone to listen to what we say as well. That means we should be able to be a listener as well as a talker. People feel they're important to you when you want to listen.

Just make sure you *really* listen. Not the kind where you focus on the person speaking but your mind is on when Jason Isaac smiled at you in chemistry.

Okay, you say, *but once I'm listening, what do I do with all the secret info?* Ooh. Good question.

A genuine friend is one who can be trusted. When Josh tells you in confidence that he likes Bethany, you can't run off and tell her—even though it'll kill you not to. On the other hand, if your friend is in danger of hurting herself or someone else, you can't keep that information private. But for the most part, keeping secrets is being trustworthy.

It's just as important to *talk* as it is to listen. The key is learning *when.* Never talk just to hear yourself talk—like my friend who just talked *all* the time. But also, don't put the burden of the entire conversation on someone else. You've got to do your part too.

Okay, you're saying, *but what if sometimes I just don't know what to say?*

Here's a little secret: If you're really listening to what the other person is saying, you'll have questions.

For example, Eric just mentioned he has a lot of math homework. Your question might be: "Do you like math?"

"Ah, it's okay. But Mrs. Johnson sure gives us a lot of homework!"

"I haven't had Mrs. Johnson. Is she a good teacher?"

When you're out of questions throw in your own thoughts: "Do you like English? I've got a huge report to write on this play we've been reading in Lit."

Even if you know the person really well, asking questions and adding your own comments helps you get to know the person even better.

Be yourself

Emma was really frustrated! Hannah's dad was totally rich, and almost every week it seemed Hannah was making more friends because of what she wore to school: $120 jeans, a $400 jacket, $300 shoes!

Emma couldn't keep up. Finally, she decided to simply be herself. She decided to stop trying to be like Hannah—or anyone else. She was going to wear what she liked.

Of the ones who noticed her when she walked into school Monday morning, Hannah was the most expressive.

"Emma! Where did you find that outfit! The Salvation Army?" People around her laughed.

"No. I've just decided to wear what I like, that's all."

"If you like that, you do have problems."

Emma ignored the snickers behind her. She closed her locker and flashed Hannah a genuine smile. "Don't worry, Hannah. We can still be friends because I know my fancy clothes don't make me any better than you. Fashion isn't everything."

Think it's hard to become a trendsetter? It's not. Anything can be "in" when you wear it with confidence and decide to be yourself.

So ask yourself: Am I being *me,* or am I imitating others? God created you in His image. He made you unique. He didn't make you a copy; why copy anyone else?

Often, it's the people who try to imitate others who are afraid to be themselves. "Fear not, for I have redeemed you; I have summoned you by name; you are mine" (Isaiah 43:1). If God Himself chooses us and calls us by name, what could we possibly have to fear? When we realize that the King of Kings accepts us and loves us just as we are, we are set free from ever having to impress, follow, or imitate anyone.

Add value to those around you

Find something good in each of your family members and encourage them. Look for people who go the extra mile for others, and tell them you notice. Watch those who are shy and highlight their tender spirits. When you affirm someone and add value to what they do well, you'll be amazed to see how they respond!

Following those five strategies will make you friends. Guaranteed. And there's just one more thing.

Wait! You said five strategies!

I know, I know. But this is the most important one, I promise.

Before I tell you what it is, I need to tell you in all honesty that it may not really help you make friends. In fact, you might even lose a few because of it. But that doesn't mean it's not the most important thing you can do.

Ready? Here it is:

Be Jesus to those around you

Jesus depends on us to be His hands, feet, arms, ears. Are you using your hands, feet, arms, and ears to bring glory to Him? Are you going the extra mile for someone who needs you? When your friends are hurting, do you love them? When Julie battles an eating disorder, can you comfort and advise her? When Brooke shares that she's been abused, when Geoff confides that his parents are splitting, or Austin tells you that his mother is dying of cancer—they don't need a bunch of pat Christian phrases. They need Jesus.

At times Jesus loved with "tough love." He never made excuses if someone was trapped in sin. He didn't say, "Oh, you're sinning? Well, that's okay. You didn't mean it. I'll just go ahead and forget it." He forgave but He allowed people to feel the conviction of the Holy Spirit for their disobedience. And still, He never condemned. He always continued to love people just the way they were.

When your friends are battling deep scars, don't make excuses. Don't try to lessen their responsibility. Just love them like Jesus would. Sometimes that will mean giving a hug. Sometimes it will mean telling them just what they need to hear—even something they don't want to hear like, "I'll back you up when you're ready to accept your responsibility."

Being Jesus to your friends is not easy. Jesus didn't always do the popular thing—He just did what was right for the person. And we both know that sometimes doing what's right costs some popularity. God doesn't ask you to be popular, just sincere. He may not provide you with a great stage and a microphone with which to do it. But He is calling you to serve. Be His love to a lost and dying world.

*Adapted from the book *Help! My Friend's in Trouble* by Susie Shellenberger, published by Servant Publications. ©2000. Used with permission.

"The Best Way to Have a Friend Is to Be One"

Follow these tips toward making new friendships:

- Risk and reach out. Invite that new girl to your youth group.

- Look for the lonely. There's always someone needing a friend.

- Always ask. Questions give people a chance to talk. Listen.

- Practice patience. It takes time to build a solid friendship.

- Be realistic. Not everyone will like you. Don't take it personally.

When to End a Friendship

Aimee looked over her shoulder. The salesman was busy helping a new employee with the cash register. The coast was clear. She unbuttoned her coat and grabbed the silver-looped earrings, stuffing them in her pocket.

"Aimee," Meredith whispered. "What are you doing?"

"Shhh!" Aimee said. "Just be cool." Meredith watched as her friend Aimee buttoned her coat and quietly left the store.

Imagine you're Meredith. What do you do? (Notice, we're not asking what you *should* do . . . we're asking what you *would* do.) Take a few minutes to think about it.

You have several options:

- Scream, "Citizen's arrest! Stop in the name of the public!"

- Ignore her and follow to see where she goes.

- Go for a karate chop to the hand followed by a roundhouse kick to the head.

- Offer to pick out a nice diamond pendant to go with her earrings.

The list could go on, right? You could even decide to stop being her friend . . . or at least stop letting her "borrow" your stuff. Which brings us to an all-important question: When should you end a friendship?

Quick answer? *When you're being negatively influenced.*

Easy enough, right? Well, not really. Let's talk a bit about what that really means.

Friends Are a Reflection

Ever heard "Birds of a feather flock together"? There's truth in that. You never see eagles hanging out with sparrows. When you're deciding with whom you want to develop friendships, you're making an incredibly important decision. Your choice will reflect who you are. You're not going to choose someone who hates you. Chances are, you'll choose someone who shares common interests, affirms you, someone you enjoy. To a degree, the person echoes who you are.

So if you're not into slasher movies, you don't really want to be close friends with a girl who quotes all the lines and hangs the movie posters in her locker. If you don't swear and drink you wouldn't want to become best friends with those who do. There needs to be deeper common ground. When you're close friends with people who don't share your values, there's always the danger others will assume you're like them. When they see you hanging out together, you will be "guilty by association."

So how do I get the friends I want?

This one's easy to answer. Think about the kind of friend you'd love to have and then be that person. If trust is important to you, be trustworthy. You want someone to laugh with and who enjoys good jokes? Be willing to laugh at yourself, show someone you're willing to risk embarrassment for a good laugh.

Curtain Call

So getting back to Aimee the thief, let's say you and Aimee have been friends for a year. You've invited her to church, but she won't come. She knows you don't approve of her actions. In other words, it's clear that you're probably not going to be the person to lead her to Christ. Here's the hard part: You need to trust God to let someone else do that. You've planted some powerful seeds, but Aimee isn't going to let you pray with her, and she certainly isn't about to change her lifestyle. And maybe your mom's noticed you developing strange behaviors that aren't you. Aimee's being a bad influence on you. Instead of you drawing Aimee to Christ, she's drawing you farther away from Him.

Make your friendship with Aimee a matter of prayer. Ask God to either soften Aimee's heart so you can lead her to Him, or give you the strength to back away from the friendship. And if that seems kind of cold, remember: You've been friends with her for a year. She knows where you stand. And your goal is to glorify God. If you're not able to draw your friends to Christ, they might draw you from Him.

There will be times, though, when a friend is sinning but is not having a negative influence on you. Too often we abandon friends who are on the wrong path, when God may use an enduring and unconditionally loving friendship to ultimately bring someone back. You'll have to determine whether you are having a positive influence on your friend or she is dragging you down. Seek advice from your mom or a mature friend who might see the situation more clearly than you can.

When Jesus walked the earth, He took time to invest in close friendships. He knows how important friends are, and He wants you to have friends too. But He wants you to have real, meaningful friendships. Seek His guidance when making friends. Allow Him to be your best friend, and all your other friends will want to know Him too.

How to Help a Friend

Sometimes people will try anything to be popular. They compromise once, then twice . . . and before they know it . . . they're in trouble—and they might not even realize it. All they can think about is being cool.

Know someone who's slipping? Here's how you can help:

- Get advice from your parents or youth leader.

- Read what the Bible says on helping others and ask Jesus to show you what to do.

- Find time to talk.

- Listen to what your friend says. If she asks for something that makes you uncomfortable, be careful. Share advice, not assistance. And don't push.

- Even if your friend withdraws, keep being a friend. What she needs most is someone who cares. Eventually, she might figure that out.

- Ask God to help you love/forgive her. If you've tried everything and you're only getting more worried, the most loving thing you can do is to let an adult know. Your friend will be upset, but at least she'll be alive to thank you later.

Handling Peer Pressure

"Hey, Kacie! You going to the party Friday night at Brandon's?"

"I'm not planning on it."

"You're kidding! Brandon's parents are gone for the entire weekend! Everyone's gonna be there! And you're not going?"

"Yeah, everyone's going to be there with no parents around. That's why I'm not going."

"Huh? What are you *talking* about?!"

"Come on. No adults? No one to take responsibility for all the stuff that could happen? I don't wanna put myself in that kind of situation."

"You're talking crazy. When else are you gonna get this kind of opportunity?"

"What opportunity? To sit around a bunch of drunk guys with one thing on their minds? No thanks. Doesn't sound tempting to me. To smoke something that could get me wasted, in jail, or severely messed up? I just don't need to be a part of all that."

"Whatever, girl! It's not like anyone's going to force you to smoke or drink! You can do what you want! It doesn't mean you don't have to go! You have to come—it's like, your duty as a wild woman! What's the point of being a teenager if you can't have some reckless fun?"

Pause for a minute here and think about which one of these girls you admire. Which one do you think is doing something smart and meaningful this weekend? What if every teen could keep their cool when faced with this kind of pressure? What's Kacie's secret?

We don't have to tell you about the kind of pressure you face as a teenager. What you do with that pressure, how you handle it, determines the kind of woman people see you as. The choice Kacie made right there will have an enormous effect on her entire life. Don't believe it? Read on.

Let's talk strategy for a second. There are strategies for any situation you can encounter. How do you handle peer pressure like this? Let's take a look at where Kacie's confidence comes from.

The Strategy

What Kacie did when she was faced with a common pressure situation was . . .

1 Think ahead.

Kacie has obviously spent time imagining problems she might encounter if she caved in to the pressure she was facing. She thought about Brandon's parents, thought about what would probably be happening without them there: drinking, maybe drugs, definitely guys and girls hooking up. Kacie made her decision well before she ever encountered the opposition. She thought ahead.

With any situation, you can do the same. You don't have to know about a particular party to know what your answer to an invitation would be. Imagine the worst-case scenario. Drugs and alcohol passing around the house and the police show up and bust everyone. Do you think it will matter to the cops whether or not you've been partaking? What will spending a night in jail do for your future? How about your dreams, your college scholarships? It pays to think ahead.

2 Visualize the repercussions.

What if you *do* give in to the pressure from your guy to go further physically? Consequences may include pregnancy, STDs, AIDS, a broken heart, damage in your personal relationship with Christ, damage to your reputation, disappointing your folks, etc.

If you can visualize the consequences ahead of time, you'll probably make the right decisions.

3 Seek direction from God.

Jesus died not only for your sins; He also died for the pressure you're facing. He's ready to give you the wisdom and guidance you need. Check this out: "If any of you lacks wisdom, he should ask God, who gives generously to all without finding fault, and it will be given to him" (James 1:5).

He wants to empower you with His strength so you can conquer the problems you encounter. You've heard this phrase over and over: "What Would Jesus Do?" When you face a problem, ask yourself this incredibly important question and wait for God's answer.

4 Do the right thing—no matter how hard.

You may be familiar with the Nike® slogan "Just Do It!" The same holds true for you. It won't be easy to go against the crowd. It won't be popular to stand alone. It'll never be cool to do what's right . . . but with God's strength surging through you, "Just Do It!"

The key, though, is to remember you can't fight temptation alone. No one can. God *wants* to help, so ask Him! And arm yourself with ammunition (Scripture). The more Scripture you have memorized, the easier it will be to fight temptation.

Pack these powerful pieces of ammo in your memory bank:

- *"No temptation has seized you except what is common to man. And God is faithful; he will not let you be tempted beyond what you can bear. But when you are tempted, he will also provide a way out so that you can stand up under it."*
  —1 Corinthians 10:13

- *"Because he himself suffered when he was tempted, he is able to help those who are being tempted."*
  —Hebrews 2:18

- *"We are hard pressed on every side, but not crushed; perplexed, but not in despair; persecuted, but not abandoned; struck down, but not destroyed."*
  —2 Corinthians 4:8-9

- *"Cast all your anxiety on him because he cares for you."*
  —1 Peter 5:7

Your Greatest Weapon

Prayer is the very best way to fight temptation, overcome peer pressure, and handle problems. So let's pray right now, okay?

Dear Jesus:

I don't know what problems I'll face tomorrow and next week or five years from now. But I know I'll need Your help. So, Jesus, right when I'm in the midst of the battle, please remind me to turn to You. I realize I can't handle my problems, and the pressure that comes with them, on my own. Help me to consistently seek Your wisdom. And when You tell me what to do, help me obey You.

Thanks, Jesus. I love You!
Amen.

Cliques: Pride or Prejudice?

"Am I now trying to win the approval of men, or of God? Or am I trying to please men? If I were still trying to please men, I would not be a servant of Christ."

—Galatians 1:10

Cliques come with the teenage territory. Whether you're in one or ostracized by one, most teens have some experience with cliques. Remove all the labels, like "jocks," "snobs," "nerds," or "weirdos," and you have two categories: those who are considered "cool" and those who aren't. It's awesome to know that popularity doesn't matter to God. It really doesn't. You could work hard every single day of your high school career to fit in, but it'll never matter. You're already worth more than life itself.

But to help you through the daily grind of school, read the following two fictional journal entries. If you ask God how you can start seeing your peers as individuals—each one worthy of respect—you may be surprised by the result.

Jenn

My parents tell me that I'm talented—that I ought to be proud that I'm one of the few who "gets" to play flute. I do love it, don't get me wrong, but I hate the classification I get because of it. At school I'm a "band nerd." Anyone who is in band is a band nerd. I pray about it, but somehow that doesn't make facing the ridicule any easier.

I love my friends and all the stuff we do together: lunch, practice, study, going to music festivals, and just hanging out. We laugh and talk deep stuff like the meaning of life. A couple of us even get together to pray once in a while. We're all pretty easy to get along with. So I just can't understand why we're being belittled every day. It's like we're suffering for having the interests and talents we have and for not caring about being cool. I mean, what if people like us were the cool people? That would be so much more realistic! We accept everyone—flaws and all.

I guess if I was honest, I'd have to admit that I wish I were popular. If for nothing else, simply for the respect! I wouldn't choose any other friends in the world over the ones I have right now. But I would readily choose to have a different reputation. Who likes being a nerd? The popular girls have it so easy . . .

Danielle

I suppose I should be thankful that I'm considered one of the "popular" girls. There are 10 of us, to be specific. They call us the Hilton Hotties. Hilton's my high school. The Hotties are us—seven cheerleaders, two soccer players, and the junior class president. I'm one of the seven in the gold and blue uniforms cheering on the sidelines every Friday night.

Being a Hottie definitely has its perks. I mean, if I wasn't in this group, my social calendar would be pretty bare. The girls outside our group rarely get asked out, they don't get invited to any of the "real" parties, and it never looks like they have much fun.

So I've got it good, huh? I mean, it sounds like I shouldn't have any worries or problems because I'm cool . . . right? The truth is that the appearance of my life may be attractive, but I feel alone in the in group more often than not.

The bottom line is that if I didn't make the squad this year, I wouldn't even be a part of this group. And so little of the whole thing has anything to do with me—the real me. It's all about looks, what you wear, surface stuff. It's sick. God doesn't care about any of it! And I really want to care more about what God thinks than what they do. But it's hard to remember that day to day.

The reality is that being popular isn't at all what it's cracked up to be. For some girls it's great. They love the attention and the ego trip—and it is a "trip" because it's not real. These girls are so insecure, I just want to cry. They don't even know what it's like to have their own opinions or to accept their real, God-given talents. They actually try to hide anything like that for the sake of fitting in.

The people I truly admire are those the other Hotties laugh at: the smart kids. They can dress however they want. The quiet ones are always more thoughtful, more real. They get trash-talked but if they stick to their beliefs, and refuse to compromise, they'll make out 10 times better than the Hotties will. They're the ones who'll make something of their lives.

God, help me have the guts to actually live all of this. I want to have one friend, just one girl, who really cares about me . . . about who I am on the inside.

Cliques, Clumps, and Cattle

Have you ever watched a herd of cattle? Cows love to stand around, eat, and chew—and hang out in a big group. Occasionally one cow will lift her head and say, "Hey girls, that grass is greener. Come on." And then the herd follows.

Look more closely, and you'll notice clumps: smaller groups of cows that hang together like mini-herds of their own.

It's true of cows just as it's true of teens. We hang out with the few that we have the most in common with and it doesn't take long before the rest of the herd slaps a label on us.

It's normal to hang out with people who have common interests, goals, and beliefs. Those things naturally draw us together and give a foundation for friendship. The problem comes when we get exclusive and keep only to ourselves. Sure, it's important to choose good friends wisely, but God has also called us to reach out and love the world. That's how they'll see the difference in us.

So ask yourself these questions to see if you're stuck in a clique.

- Do you talk with others who hang in different groups?

- When was the last time you and your buds added a new member to your group?

- Do you spend as much time watching for new guys and girls to get to know as you do trying to get noticed?

- In the past week, have you said hello to somebody you don't know well?

- Can you name five friends who aren't a part of your group at school?

Jealousy, the Monster

Dear Diary,

It happened again. I had one jealous moment after another tonight. It started when I arrived at youth group early and saw Collin talking to Sara. I know he doesn't like me or anything, but for some reason I get jealous when I see him talking to other girls.

Then Tracey pulled up in her new car—the one her parents bought her. I couldn't help thinking it wasn't fair I got the hand-me-down pickup truck from my brother.

I thought my attitude might change once the evening began, but when I saw one of my closest friends search out two other girls to sit with during worship, I couldn't keep the tears away. I still don't know why she didn't ask me to sit with them.

I'm so tired of feeling this way. I'm tired of comparing myself to others. God, what am I supposed to do? How do I get past all of this jealousy? Forgive me for these wrong feelings . . . again.

Samantha

Who Is This Monster, Anyway?

Often dubbed "the green-eyed monster," jealousy is one of the ugliest faces of sin—and it's a common occurrence among teen girls. It's a product of our flesh and has nothing to do with life in the Spirit of God. Jealousy shows its ugliness when you begin to compare yourself to others and when you feel you don't have everything you deserve.

Consider Samantha. She wanted attention from Collin, wasn't getting it, and became jealous. She compared her truck to Tracey's car, *believed* she deserved something better, and became jealous again.

Jealousy is *believing* something is wrong with the picture. Life isn't playing fair.

Bringing the Monster Down

Notice how Samantha reached the point of jealousy over and over when she decided to believe certain things, even without the basis of truth. To bring jealousy down, you need to evaluate your beliefs. Is there an area where you believe you've been slighted, overlooked, left out? Do you regularly compare yourself, your possessions, or your situation to others'?

Now, what do you really believe about your friends, family, classmates, and God? Do you think they like you? Do you think they would really intentionally hurt you? Do you believe God doesn't have your best interests in mind all the time?

What you choose to believe will affect how you live. If you believe people don't like you, you'll think less of yourself. If you believe you've been slighted, you'll desire what others have which makes you more prone to think you deserve what others have. But if you believe God has a plan for your life, you'll trust Him.

Finding a New Identity

Living with jealousy is no fun. There's no freedom there; no room to be lighthearted, or to be happy for others and their blessings. If you've been wearing the mask of the green-eyed monster, it's time to find a new identity.

Begin with who you are in Christ. Ask God to strip away the jealousy in your heart and to shape you into the likeness of Jesus. God is love, and as 1 Corinthians 13:4 tells us, "Love does not envy."

Ask God to show you how to turn toward love when you start to feel jealous. Love, as opposed to jealousy, is trusting God to provide what you need when you need it, and rejoicing in God's blessings—no matter who the recipient is.

Next, think back to the answers you gave for the questions in the previous section. Truly consider your beliefs. If you believe things that are not true—about yourself, others, or God—find out what is true, and adjust accordingly.

If it goes unchecked, jealousy will interfere in your relationships with God, your family, and your friends. So get rid of the monster and let God bestow His blessings on you in His own time.

School Daze

During your four years of high school, you will spend over 4,000 hours of your life in class (that's assuming you make it to class). It may be tempting to think of those 4,000 hours as time that you're *forced* to be there, but actually paying attention during that time can produce great dividends, not just in grades and academic knowledge, but in the increase of self-discipline.

And who knows? Someday when you're facing Alex Trebek or Regis Philbin, something that your third period teacher once said may actually come back to help you win significant dollars! The truth is that school is far more than learning head knowledge; it is a training ground for characteristics and skills that can create a lifestyle that is satisfying whether college fits into your plans at all.

Want to make those 4,000 hours count? Keep reading.

The ABCs of School Success

Yeah, we know. School isn't always a breeze. Sometimes it's downright hard. And it's easy to get frustrated when you fail a test, forget your homework, or hate the class.

Hold on! We'd love to help. No, we can't do your algebra homework for you . . . so don't even *think* about sending it to us! But we can offer some super-cool tips that really work. But this one's kind of long. So before you get started, grab some popcorn and a tall glass of lemonade and meet us back here in four minutes, okay?

All right, let's dive in!

A Attitude

Yeah, it really is important. If you walk into English class thinking, *Gross! I hate this class. I hate this subject. I'd rather have a root canal than study this boring stuff,* your teacher will pick up on that. I know, because I used to be a high school teacher. And we really do know everything! (Okay, not really . . . but when a student has a negative attitude, it shows!) So decide right now to change your negative thoughts into positive ones. Go ahead. Think of two positive things about the class you hate the most and jot them in the space provided. I'll give you some examples to get you started:

- The teacher doesn't make me eat liver during class.

- In one year, it'll all be over. I can handle anything for just one year.

- This class must be important or I wouldn't have to take it.

- (Okay, your turn.)

C Cultivate good study habits

And that means being consistent. Do your homework the first chance you get, study a little each day, and go over your class notes regularly. Sound too easy? Those three simple steps will help you establish solid study habits that will take you right through college!

D Discover

Make it your goal to learn at least one new thing every day. If you walk into school actively seeking something new, you'll find it. And you'll be surprised how much this will help with the first thing we talked about—attitude.

E Excellence

Strive for excellence. Determine not to take short-cuts. Does this mean everything you do will always be perfect? No. But when you place your energy and focus on striving for excellence, you'll find yourself studying a little more and willing to go the extra mile. Know what that means? Your teacher will notice. And there's not a teacher in the world who doesn't respect a student who's striving to do the best she can do.

B Breakfast

You've already heard that breakfast is the most important meal of the day. So make time for it! It's a well-known fact that students who have something nutritious in their system early in the morning are more alert, think faster, and *feel* better physically and emotionally. Reread that last sentence, okay? There's a key word we want you to zero in on. It's *nutritious*. So gum doesn't count. Neither do Lifesavers. We're talking cereal or a bagel or some eggs or a piece of toast or some fruit—you know—*real* food. Try it consistently for one month. You'll be surprised at the positive difference it makes!

F Feed yourself

We've already covered breakfast. But your mind needs feeding as well. Make time to watch the news, read up on current events, dive into a book when it's not an assignment. These are ways to sharpen your thinking outside of the classroom.

G Gather everything you need

As a former teacher, one of the most frustrating things I faced every day was the student who never had what she needed.

"Can I borrow a pencil?"

"Anyone got an extra sheet of paper?"

"I forgot my book."

A teacher quickly loses respect for someone who's never prepared. Make a mental list of everything you need for each class and walk in prepared—every day.

H Help!

If you don't understand something, don't be afraid to ask for help. And if there's not enough time for your teacher to give you personal attention during class, ask afterward if there's a time when you can drop by to ask questions.

I Importance

It's easy to get distracted in school and think what you're studying isn't important. Not only is school important, but you are important as well! Repeat after me: "I am important. What I'm learning is important. And what I'm doing is important."

Repeat it again—this time out loud. (Go ahead. No one's listening.)

You didn't do it, did you?

Well, we can't go on until you do.

So take a deep breath and read it out loud . . . *with meaning:* "I am important. What I'm learning is important. And what I'm doing is important."

Whew. Glad we got through that. Need more ice in your lemonade? Take a break for a refill, and meet me back here in one minute.

J Jawbreaker

They're good, aren't they? Especially the fireball red-hot cinnamon ones! But there's a trick to eating jawbreakers. And this is where patience comes in. If you let the candy sit in your mouth, slowly savoring its sweetness, you'll enjoy it to the point where you can finally bite into it and get the deep flavor. But if you bite into it immediately, you're likely to break a tooth and miss *all* the flavor!

Some classes are like jawbreakers. It can take an entire semester for geometry to start to sink in. But once it does, it all begins to click. Don't get frustrated too quickly! You may be trying to bite when you should be willing to listen, take notes, and savor the lessons—letting them sink in over time. By doing that, you'll eventually get to the flavor. We promise!

K — Know-it-all

No one likes him. He's the guy in every class who's convinced himself he knows more than the teacher. Guess what—there may be a class in which you actually do know more than the teacher! If you've been playing the piano since you were four, chances are you may know more than your band teacher who only plays trumpet and tuba. But that doesn't give you license to strut your stuff. You can still learn from him. That's right—there's always an opportunity to learn from any teacher!

The most valuable quality a teacher looks for in all students is *teachability*. As a former high school drama teacher, I often cast the less talented students in lead acting roles simply because they were teachable. Many times the more talented students thought they knew it all, and it was extremely difficult to convince them to try the scene another way. They weren't flexible.

Teachability. It's something know-it-alls don't have. But it's something every teacher values.

L — Listen!

This quality goes with the last one. If I could stress one thing it would be to listen.

"What page?"

"Is this gonna be on the test?"

"Can you say that again?"

It's important to ask questions when you don't understand. But if you listen, most of the time a teacher will end up answering your questions by the end of class. Don't frustrate your teacher by asking him or her to repeat something just said.

Remember, listening skills are acquired by not talking.

M | Meanwhile

Meanwhile is an adjective that means "during the intervening time." Think of your school years as meanwhile, intervening time. In other words, they don't last forever. Graduation will be here before you know it. If you view these years as your training period, you'll see there's light at the end of the tunnel. You're not there yet, you're just shaping yourself for the destination.

N | Nastiness

Don't talk it. Don't live it. Don't even get close to it. 'Nuff said.

O | Objection

"Your Honor, I have an objection." You don't have to agree with everything adults say simply because they hold the authority. But you do need to show you respect them.

If, for instance, your science teacher is teaching on evolution, take the opportunity to politely object. This is a great time for you to express the facts on creation and intelligent design. But before you do, you need to know your facts. Don't mouth off without having the info to back you up.

If there's good reason to object, do so. But the key word is politely.

P | Peer Pressure

Instead of succumbing to negative peer pressure, why not be the leader in turning it all around? Did you know you have the power to create positive peer pressure? Start with your lifestyle. Are you the same person at school that you are at church? God hates hypocrisy, and He wants to help you be consistent in living a godly life. So lean on Him, and live a life that screams integrity.

Others are attracted to someone who's honest, full of character, and fun to be around. And by living this kind of life, you'll be raising the standard for those around you to follow. In other words, you'll be dishing out positive peer pressure!

A great place to start is the annual "See You at the Pole" event every September. Christian students around the world gather at the flagpole of their schools on this specific day to pray for their student body and teachers. What a great way to make a statement with your life! It's also a fast way to find out who the Christians are at your school.

Get more information from: www.syatp.com.

Q Quaff

Cool word, huh? Not to be confused with "coiffure" which is French for hairstyle, quaff means "to drink deeply." Adapt this as your attitude during your school years. Refuse to be a student who simply learns enough just to get by. Instead, drink deeply. Inhale knowledge. Saturate yourself with learning. Take advantage of our educational system and quaff it for all it's worth!

R Random acts of kindness

No, it won't make you learn any faster or give you better grades. But you *will* get a reputation as a giving and thoughtful person. You can practice these toward your teachers and school administrators.

You're kidding, right?

Nope. A little kindness goes a long way. Get in the habit of randomly doing nice things for people: Leave a note on your coach's desk and let her know how much you appreciate her passion for sports. Say hi when you pass a teacher in the hallway. The key is to teach yourself the habit so it becomes natural and feels sincere.

S Smile

Remember the tips on popularity? Well, then go back and read them again!

T Tricks

Create some cool study tricks to help you remember information better. Having a tough time remembering how to spell Yoknapatawpha (the fictional setting for American author William Faulkner's stories)? Then make up a sentence beginning with each letter of the word. Here's an example. My mom taught me this in fourth grade when I had to learn how to spell **geography.**

George **E**lliot's **o**ld **g**randfather **r**ode **a p**ig **h**ome **y**esterday.

Study tricks will not only help you remember needed information, they can also make studying fun!

U Unlettered

It means "not educated. Illiterate." Which is what people will think of you if you don't take school seriously.

V Victory

Celebrate your victories. You passed that pop math quiz? Great! Hang it on the fridge. You aced the essay you were worried about? Treat yourself to a low-fat dessert. You didn't faint during your speech? Tell your parents, and ask them if you can go bowling or play a game of mini-golf!

Celebrating the times you do well will motivate you to strive for excellence after a time you don't do well. No one's perfect. You probably won't ace every test. But when you do accomplish a good mark, take time to revel in the victory!

W Work hard

Some students have to work harder than others. Be willing to study more if you need it. Work means sacrifice. So if you need to skip your favorite TV show tonight to study for your chemistry test tomorrow...remember that working hard pays off. Consistent hard work pays off even faster! By working hard now, you develop a solid work ethic to help you climb your way to the top.

X Xenophobia

Betcha don't know what this is! It's being afraid or hateful of strangers, foreigners, or anything strange or foreign.

Guess what? Your school is full of variety. And that variety shows up best in people. Is there a new student in your class this year? Go out of your way to make her feel included.

You heard there's a transfer student from Germany? Ask her to join you for lunch. You notice Marci is always by herself. "She's weird," people say. So what? Go the extra mile. Reach out. Offer to pick her up for Friday night's football game.

Know what'll happen? Not only will you prove you're not xenophobic . . . but you'll also be spreading positive peer pressure!

Y You

Do you realize how incredibly much God loves you? He cares about every single thing that concerns you! And yes, that means school. He cares about your homework. He understands when it's hard to digest trig. So talk with Him about it.

Know what else? Right now . . . while you're in school . . . He's dreaming BIG dreams for you. We dare you to memorize the proof: "Now to him who is able to do immeasurably more than all we ask or imagine" (Ephesians 3:20).

When you're faced with a difficult teacher, a tough class, and a subject you don't understand, turn to God. He wants to help!

Z Zany

Dare to be a little zany during your school years. Half the fun of going to school is having fun at school! Join a club. Participate in a crazy skit. Dress up on costume day.

Being zany won't make you a better student, but it will help you have fun. And fun is what good memories are made of. We know deep inside, you're looking forward to the day when you can tell your grandchildren about the time you dressed as a carrot to give your oral report on vegetables in speech class!

Relating to Teachers

Let's take a moment to undo one commonly believed rumor: Teachers are NOT (repeat, ARE NOT) aliens from another planet. Nor are they robots with no recognizable human characteristics. In fact, hard as it may be to believe, they are human beings. And their purpose is truly to work for your benefit.

Now that they have been humanized, here are a few things NOT to do to teachers if you want to get along with them:

1. Don't make fun of them.

2. Don't expect them to do you favors (that doesn't mean they won't do them; just don't expect them).

3. Don't question their authority in the classroom.

4. Don't write out a slip sending them to the office.

5. Don't fall asleep while they are talking to the class.

6. Don't flirt with them (even if he is cute and young).

7. Don't try to confuse them when the principal is in the room.

8. Don't treat them like buddies.

9. Don't neglect to do assignments they give because the assignments seem like busy work to you.

10. Don't use church activities as an excuse even if they go to your church.

Here's the truth about teachers: You will get along with some of them and will have trouble getting along with others. You see, this is like the real world. Those of you who already have jobs realize that some supervisors are easier to please than others, some are more helpful than others, some are old, some are young, some are easy-going, and others are all business. Teachers are the same way—fitting all of those categories. Some work hard (in fact, I would say most) and get a little ruffled when non-educators say, "You only work nine months a year from eight to three with all those vacations."

For students (and this will hold through into college as well), teachers are put into authority over you by God, so there are some verses in Romans that you should be familiar with and should apply to your life. Check out what Paul wrote to the Romans in chapter 13: "Everyone must submit himself to the governing authorities, for there is no authority except that which God has established. . . . Do you want to be free from fear of the one who is in authority? Then do what is right and he will commend you. For he is God's servant to do you good" (verses 1, 3, and 4). Some take that authority much more seriously than others and hold it tightly, but whether the teacher demands respect or not, give it to him or her. This holds true whether you attend a public school or a Christian one— and home-schooled students get a double dose because of God's command to honor your father and your mother.

Anybody who's been in schools at all realizes there are some teachers in any setting who are ripe for teasing and making fun of. Resist that temptation. In fact, whether it's a teacher or the downtrodden victimized student in the locker next to you, making fun of anyone may get you some momentary laughs, but the long-term effects result in hurt.

That "favor" part in number 2? Some teachers can be taken advantage of, but doing so may not benefit you in the long run. If it happens too often, the teacher starts to regard the favor-asker as irresponsible, a slacker who doesn't want to follow the rules set for the rest of the class. This can prove to be a particular temptation if you have a Christian teacher in a public school—don't get roped in.

But instead of focusing on what not to do to get on the good side of teachers, how can you positively approach them to contribute to your success? Six things:

- **Do your work.** Put forth your best effort instead of making excuses.

- **Ask questions.** If you don't understand something, get help from the teacher soon instead of waiting for several days or weeks. And ask questions before or after class or during a teacher's conference period. Don't interrupt the class with a question unless you think it might be something that would benefit many of your classmates—not just you.

- **Pay attention.** We're not just talking here about the falling asleep part above—pay attention to what is going on in your teachers' lives. They are people like you with good days and bad. One teacher told us, "A particular student made a dramatic impact on me when my mom was dying. I didn't make a big deal about it, but his sensitivity clued him in that I was going through a tough time. He discreetly asked me after class how I was doing—with a sincere interest. I didn't dump all my pain on him, but I felt safe to let him into my life at least a little. Knowing that he knew helped me through the next difficult couple weeks."

- **Pray for them.** Yes, just like any other people who can make a difference in your life, teachers deserve and desire your prayers.

- **Be a leader in the classroom.** Notice that doesn't say cheerleader—doing this too much can create the image of a shmoozer or a kiss-up. But you can take the responsibility to contribute to discussions, to discourage kids that act up, to use the opportunity to team with the teacher in focusing on what is being taught.

- **Stay in touch.** Even though doing so may contribute little to your school success, keep contact with teachers who have an impact in your life. Too often educators invest heavily into someone and have no idea what happens to her after graduation.

Prayer: Know Your Rights

We've talked about school success and people success, but to truly survive the chalkboard jungle, you need to know how to experience faith success as well, particularly those of you who attend public schools. The press tries to communicate that the campus is off limits to any expressions of Christian faith. But do you know what? That's not true. Constitutions of both the United States and Canada protect your freedom of religious expression. You can tell people what you believe without getting arrested! Do you know what you can and cannot do on a public school campus?

Take This Quick Quiz.

Yes	No	(Check one box per statement.)
☐	☐	**a.** Students can pray.
☐	☐	**b.** Students can read their Bibles.
☐	☐	**c.** Students can form religious clubs if other non-curricular clubs exist.
☐	☐	**d.** Students can hand out tracts, fliers, or other religious materials.
☐	☐	**e.** Students can do research papers and speeches with religious themes.
☐	☐	**f.** Students can be exempt from participating in assignments contrary to their religious beliefs.
☐	☐	**g.** Students can discuss religious issues although other students may overhear.

The answer to all of these statements is yes—students have great freedom of religious expression even on public school campuses.

Students' Bill of Rights (on a Public School Campus)

1. **The Right to Meet** with other religious students. The Equal Access Act allows students the freedom to meet on campus to discuss religious issues.

2. **The Right to Identify** your religious beliefs through signs and symbols.

3. **The Right to Talk** about your religious beliefs on campus.

4. **The Right to Distribute** religious literature on campus.

5. **The Right to Pray** on campus. Students may pray alone or with others so long as it does not disrupt school activities or is not forced on others.

6. **The Right to Carry or study** your Bible on campus. The Supreme Court of the United States has said that only state-directed Bible reading is unconstitutional.

7. **The Right to do** research papers, speeches, or creative projects with religious themes.

8. **The Right to Be Exempt.** Students may be exempt from activities and class content that contradict their religious beliefs.

9. **The Right to Celebrate** or study religious holidays on campus. Music, art, literature, or drama with religious themes are permitted if presented objectively as part of the tradition of the holiday.

10. **The Right to Meet** with school officials. The First Amendment forbids Congress to make any law that would restrict the right of the people to petition the government, including school officials.

*To learn more, request *Students' Legal Rights on a Public School Campus* ($10 U.S.), See You at the Pole, P.O. Box 60134, Fort Worth, Texas 76115. Or call 1-817-HIS-PLAN.

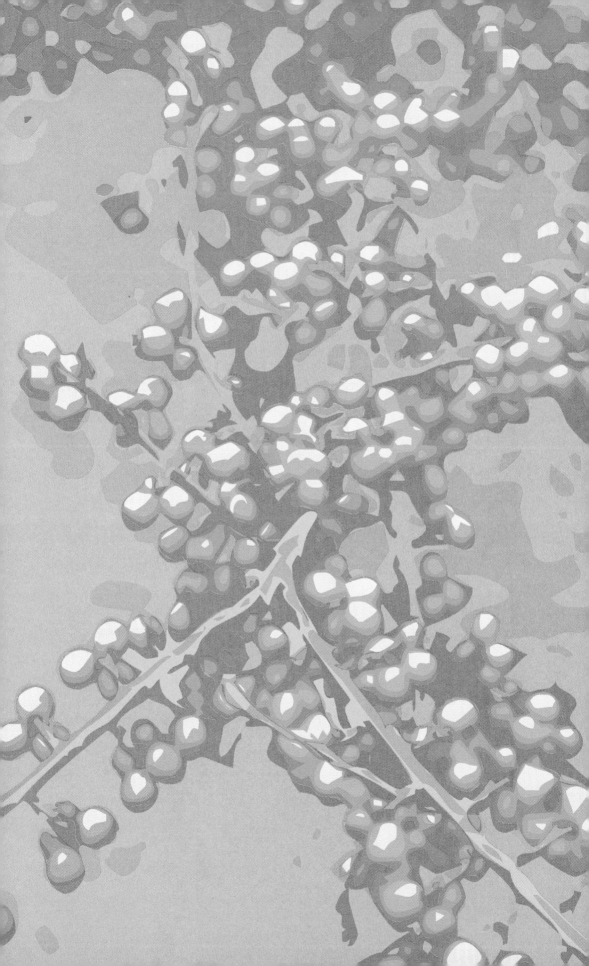

Part Four Grow Your Soul

Get a Life!

You've heard a lot about God . . . but do you know Him personally?

Erica had almost reached the dock when she heard the familiar camp bell announce the upcoming afternoon chapel. *First bell,* Erica thought. *That means I've got five minutes to get outta this canoe and up the hill.*

"Hey, Erica! Lemme help," greeted Ryan as he grabbed her paddle and helped straighten out the canoe.

"Thanks, Ry. I think I'll be ready for the race tomorrow. I just rounded the bend in less than two minutes."

"All right! We're gonna squash the Scorpions! And it's about time. They've beat us for the last two summers!"

"Yeah! Less than two minutes—can you believe it?"

"And that's about how much time we've got to get to chapel," Ryan said as the two raced up the hill.

"Guys! Over here!" Tasha said as she made room on the stone bench for her friends. Erica and Ryan hurried into the outdoor amphitheater-style chapel they had grown to love over the years. *Ah . . . this is it,* Erica thought as she took a deep breath. Yep, the sun was blistering—almost a hundred today—lots of humidity, the smell of pine, and the sound of the lake nearby. *Perfect,* she thought. *Just the way I like it. Nothing beats camp!*

The praise and worship team launched into some of Erica's favorites, and she grinned as her friends tried to pressure her into doing silly song motions on stage. She looked around. *I love this place,* she thought. *I've been coming here for eight years, and I wouldn't miss it.* She knew every song, every game, every inch of the campground. It was easy to feel this was exactly where she belonged.

Erica sat glued to the stone bench—sweat dripping off her legs—as the camp speaker began the afternoon message. During her many years of camp experience, she'd heard it all—speaker after speaker—all proclaiming God's Truth. Just as her mind began to drift to the upcoming canoe races, Erica's thoughts were startled.

"Many of you have been coming to church camp for years," the speaker said. He seemed to look right at Erica. *Hey, this guy's different,* she found herself thinking. *No middle-aged man telling corny jokes to try to catch our attention. His countenance seems different—instead of trying to impress us with pretending to be cool, he seems to simply want to get his message across.*

Erica glanced around the outdoor chapel and noticed that everyone else was glued to the speaker as well.

"But guess what, campers?" the speaker continued, "coming to church camp doesn't make you a Christian. In fact, going to church doesn't even make you a Christian!"

Erica felt confused.

"You may even be great teens doing great things. You might be from a Christian family, and you may hang out with Christian friends. But guess what? That doesn't make you a Christian."

Erica nervously shifted her weight on the stone bench. She tried to think about horseback riding, but she couldn't take her eyes off of the speaker.

"Some of you have even been baptized. I have news for you—that doesn't make you a Christian. Water never saved anyone. Several people have been baptized who aren't really Christians."

Okay, Erica thought. *Now this guy's starting to get on my nerves. Yeah, he's a good speaker . . . but who does he think he is saying stuff like this. I'm a great girl. And I've gone to church all my life. I love my Christian family. So . . . what's the deal?*

"You're not a Christian," the speaker continued, "until you've actually repented of your sins and asked Jesus Christ to come into your life."

Hey, wait a sec! Erica thought. *Is he suggesting that I'm not a Christian?*

"You may *think* you're a Christian because you do some of the things Christians do— maybe you're involved in a youth group, read your Bible, go to Sunday school. But these outward activities don't make you a Christian. And if you're not a Christian . . ." the speaker paused, "well, . . . you're headed for hell."

Whoa! Erica thought. *That's pretty heavy! Hell?!?*

"There's probably no one here who wants to talk about hell," the speaker continued. "You hear the word hell, but only used as a curse word or slang talk. You can't even watch a 30-minute TV show without hearing it used this way. But God never intended for hell to be used as slang. He intended for you to hear about it as a real place where nonbelievers will spend eternity without Him.

"And the truth is, all of us only have two choices: heaven or hell. Everyone will spend eternity in one of these two places. You'll either be with God forever, or you'll be separated from Him forever. And by remaining neutral—by not actively choosing to follow Jesus—you've cast your choice to follow the world and spend eternity in hell."

Good grief! This guy really has his nerve, Erica thought. *Where does he get off suggesting that I'm not a Christian? I come to church camp every summer, I went on a missions trip with our youth group last month. I even helped start the Christian club at school! Surely I'm a Christian! I mean . . . I'm a totally terrific girl!*

"It's not fun to talk about hell. I'd much rather tell cool stories or make you laugh, but I care about you too much to let you leave camp without hearing God's absolute truth. What we're talking about this afternoon comes straight from the Bible.

"Someone look up 'Romans 3:23' for me." Tasha stood and began reading: " For all have sinned and fall short of the glory of God."

"That means none of us is perfect," he continued. "We were born with sin. And here's the dilemma: We serve a perfect God. He cannot and will not tolerate sin in His kingdom. Does that mean we're all headed for hell? Are we all doomed because of sin? Yes—unless we seek His forgiveness and accept His gift of everlasting life.

"You heard right—it's a gift. We can't earn it, and no one deserves it. Now turn to Romans 6:23, and someone stand and read it for us, okay?"

Erica was surprised to hear Ryan stand and boldly read:

" 'For the wages of sin is death, but the gift of God is eternal life in Christ Jesus our Lord.' "

"Good news, isn't it? Christ died in our place and offers us everlasting life instead of the death we deserve. Ryan, read Romans 3:24 for us, will you?"

" '. . . and are justified freely by his grace through the redemption that came by Christ Jesus.' "

"I'm willing to guess that everyone here believes that—you believe in God and believe that Christ died for your sins. I'll bet you even believe that He conquered death and is alive right now! But guess what? That doesn't make you a Christian. Anyone can believe in God. Even Satan believes in God!

"Christianity is way more than believing in God. Someone else stand and read 1 John 1:8-9 for us."

Jessica quickly flipped the pages in her Bible and stood. " 'If we claim to be without sin, we deceive ourselves and the truth is not in us. If we confess our sins, he is faithful and just and will forgive us our sins and purify us from all unrighteousness.' "

"Think about it, will you? Before you leave camp this week, think seriously about where you stand with Jesus Christ. You've heard the facts—straight from the Bible—now it's up to you to make the decision that will affect your eternity."

Wow! Erica thought. *I can't believe it. All these years I thought I was a Christian. But now that I think about it . . . I've never truly asked Christ to come into my life. Yeah, I'm a good teen . . . but I've never repented of my sin.*

"Today, you could make the wisest decision you'll ever make by choosing to follow Christ."

The speaker's words were still echoing in Erica's head when Ryan said, "As soon as chapel is finished, let's run to the stables. I wanna make sure I get to ride Paint."

"Go on without me," Erica said. "I'll meet you there. I need to talk with God first."

What About You?

Are you *really* a Christian? Or, perhaps like
Erica, do you know a lot about Christ
without really knowing Him on an intimate
level? There's a huge difference between
knowing about God and in walking hand in
hand with Him every single day. Head
knowledge isn't strong enough to last
eternally—but heart knowledge is.

But How Do I GROW?

And if you're already a Christian, how can you deepen your walk with God? After all, Jesus *did* say that He came to give us life *abundantly!* Why settle for simply being someone who prays and attends church when you can be a godly disciple living in vibrant union with your heavenly Father? That would be like choosing Spam over steak, wouldn't it? God dreams BIG dreams for you. (Check out Ephesians 3:20!)

To deepen your spiritual roots, let's use the word "grow" to create a winning strategy.

G Get with God.

It's impossible to grow closer to someone without spending time with him or her. Think about your best friends. How did you *become* best friends? By spending time together, right? You talk a lot. You hang out together. You share your concerns and your victories.

Guess what? When you do the same with God, it's called prayer. And the more you pray, the closer you'll grow to Christ. The cool thing about praying is that God can't wait to listen! Do you realize that He cares about every single thing in your life? Believe it! He's just as concerned about an overseas famine as He is in helping you resolve the conflict with your folks. So talk to Him—about *everything.* And don't forget to listen.

Getting with God also involves going to church and finding a ministry (instead of sitting on the back row and leaving as soon as the service is over). Find a place to serve: Help in the nursery, become a greeter, join a Bible study, get involved!

R Read the Bible.

Don't you love getting a note during school?

Or coming home to find an e-mail waiting for you? Or pulling out a special card from your mailbox? We enjoy reading our friends' messages.

God has written you an incredible letter! And He wants you to be just as excited about opening His letter as you are when you open a friend's e-mail. I know. I know. I know. I can already hear your thoughts: *But I don't have time to read the Bible for an hour every day. And besides, it's boring!*

Okay, let's get a couple of things straight. You don't have to read the Bible an hour every day to grow spiritually. In fact, if you're not in the habit of reading your Bible consistently, I suggest you start with an easy goal: Read your Bible for one minute every day.

One minute?!?!

Yep. One minute. Anyone can do that. Make a pledge to God that you'll spend at least one minute everyday reading the Bible and at least one minute every day talking with Him. After you've been successful for a month, increase your goal—go for two minutes! By the end of the first couple of months, you won't even be watching the clock anymore.

God's Word is like a road map for our lives. It gives us direction and answers and everything we need to live the holy life He has called us to live. And about that second argument: *The Bible is boring!* It doesn't have to be! If your Bible is boring or hard to understand, get a new Bible. There are so many cool, easy-to-read, easy-to-understand student Bibles on the market today. They're filled with eye-catching graphics and topical indexes and all kinds of super stuff! Make a trip to your local Christian bookstore and do some browsing.

O Obey His Commands.

Determine not to be a hypocrite. Knowing the right thing to do, yet not doing it, is sin. When we blatantly sin and call ourselves Christians, we're being hypocritical. God desires for you to live a genuine, authentic godly life—one void of phoniness. The best way you can do this is to simply obey Christ.

When He tells you to do something, do it. When He convicts you of something in your life, give it to Him. There's an old, old hymn we used to sing in church: "Trust and obey, for there's no other way, to be happy in Jesus, but to trust and obey."

It's that simple: Trust His leading, and obey His Holy Spirit.

W Witness to Others.

Chances are, if you knew Michael Jordan, Jennifer Aniston, or Tom Cruise, you'd make it known. When you know Jesus Christ, you're on a first-name basis with the Creator of the universe! It doesn't get any better than that! There is no one anywhere who is more important than Him. In fact, some day every single human knee will bow at His very name.

Hey, when you enter into a personal relationship with Christ, you become a child of the King. Girls, you're a princess. Act like it! Share the good news. Live confidently. Smile a lot. And when others ask you what's going on, invite them to church, pull out your Bible, be ready to share the difference He's making in your life.

And remember . . . the greatest witness is a Christ-filled life. Your actions will shout a lot louder than your words.

Look Around

Everyone in the world stands in one of three places:

Non-Christian

Stagnant Christian

Growing Christian

Of course, the non-Christian is someone who has never accepted Jesus as her personal Savior. Again, like Erica, she may know all the right words, and actually be a very good person, but without repenting of her sins and accepting God's gift of eternal life, she's headed for hell.

The stagnant Christian is someone who has accepted Christ, but for some reason, she's no longer growing spiritually. She still goes to church, still prays—perhaps not on a daily basis—and may still be doing good things, but she's "standing still" spiritually. She's not experiencing the abundant life God has in store for her.

The growing Christian is someone who has accepted Christ as her Savior and is living in radical obedience to His Lordship. She's enjoying an intimate, *growing* relationship with Jesus.

Which category do you fit in? If you're not a Christian, you can be. As stated earlier, it's a gift. Are you ready to accept it? Accepting God's gift of forgiveness and eternal life means surrendering the control of your life to Him. Will you trust yourself to the One who made you?

If you're a *stagnant Christian,* chances are you won't be stagnant for long. Jesus told us to be hot or cold. He warned that He would spit the lukewarm from His mouth. No one can remain in neutral forever. You'll either move forward into a growing, vibrant relationship with Christ, or you'll move backward and possibly abandon your faith.

If you're a growing Christian, you're experiencing the joy of true intimacy with God. Bottom line: There are facts about everything. Some facts don't count. Others do. Those that do, usually make a difference. The facts about Jesus Christ make an *eternal* difference. Have you weighed the facts? Do you know where you'll be spending eternity?

Is That It?

If you're serious about following Christ, Congrats! The Bible tells us that all of heaven is rejoicing because of your commitment. You'll still blow it now and then . . . and when you do, don't start thinking, *Well, I tried, but I just can't cut it. Guess I'm not a Christian anymore.*

Instead, ask God to forgive you. Accept His forgiveness, and get up and keep following Him. That's part of spiritual growth. (Kinda like a baby learning how to walk—you'll fall—but don't give up!) Keep walking. Keep reading the Bible. Keep spending time with God. And keep sharing your faith. You'll be surprised at how God will strengthen your spiritual muscles.

Dump Your Sin Load Often

Let's face it, we all sin. We need to ask for God's forgiveness and dump sin—which means *confession,* the simple act of admitting to God when you've sinned. "If we confess our sins, he is faithful and just and will forgive us our sins and purify us from all unrighteousness" (1 John 1:9).

Many Christians don't admit it often enough when they've sinned. Ever go to sleep praying, "Lord, if I've sinned today, please forgive me"? What is God supposed to do with that prayer?

First, unless you've been in a coma all day, you have sinned—probably dozens of times. Think of all the selfish thoughts, unkind words, and foolish acts you're capable of in 24 hours. There's no "Lord, *if* I've sinned" about it. Sin is there like black on coal. Second, confession is not something you should just do at the end of the day. Sin is best dealt with on the spot. D. L. Moody, a great evangelist, used to toss his hat in the air every time he recognized sin in his life. It was his way of saying, "Thanks, Jesus, for forgiving me again."

Third, confessing sin requires getting specific. What exactly did you do wrong?

Finally, confessing often is reaffirming. Why? Confession leads to the realization: "Lord, I wasn't living your life right there. Take over again. Let Your life be my life." If you pray it 1,000 times a day that just means you get 1,000 reminders that Jesus' life is the only life worth living every day.

So dump away! And remember 1 John 1:9: It's impossible to wear out.

Become a Woman of Integrity

So you're a Christian and you're growing in Christ. But there's something more you need to do: build integrity. What's integrity? Webster's describes it as "uncompromising adherence to moral and ethical principles." Wow. That's a heavy definition. What does it mean in the real world?

Take This Quick Quiz.

What now? (Check one box per question.)

You witness a stranger shoplifting at the mall. You:

☐ **a.** tell the store manager, or

☐ **b.** pretend you didn't see anything.

Your best friend shoplifts while hanging out at the mall with you. You:

☐ **a.** confront her and tell the store manager, or

☐ **b.** confront her and promise to keep the secret.

You leave your favorite clothing store and realize the clerk gave you a $10 bill instead of a $1 bill in change. You:

☐ **a.** go back and get the correct change, or

☐ **b.** count this your lucky day and keep it.

The above "shopping honesty quiz" makes it pretty easy to determine what sets a girl with integrity apart from a girl who will compromise when she doesn't want to create any waves. (In case you didn't notice, all A's makes the grade. B answers scream: *integrity problem!*)

But let's complicate matters a bit. Life is rarely as cut and dried as we wish it could be—especially in the area of what's right and wrong.

Take your best friend, Katie, for example. She lets you in on a secret. The prom is coming up and she would absolutely die if Marc asked her out. But no one, not even her *dog,* knows she likes Marc. You promise that juicy tidbit will stay between you and her; that no one will *ever* find out.

Well, Marc sits by you in science one day. You had no idea that he'd sigh under his breath that he really wants to ask someone to the prom, but he just doesn't know who. You're presented with a wide open door. You simply say, "Aren't you and Katie in English together? You two would totally have fun at the prom!"

Innocent, suave, well-intended . . . nice work.

But he zeros in on you, stares into your eyes like a hawk, and asks, "Does she like me?" Of course, you freeze. You can't tell a lie! But you can't forget your promise.

"Um," you say.

BOOM! He's got his answer and you didn't even have to say anything. You may as well have just blurted it out to the entire class for all the good you did saying, "Um." Now Katie will know that you blabbed! In no time, you've accidentally shattered your promise. Did the good you were intending outweigh the costs of breaking your promise? Did the end justify the means?

Life never stops throwing tricky situations
your way. Situations where you, being the
upright and moral person you are, are pressed
to make a decision. Right won't feel as right
as it would have before you assessed all of
the variables. Wrong won't be easy to
pinpoint. It will even look good, possibly
better than choosing the right thing!

So what's a girl to do? How do you become a
person of integrity?

Each time you're struggling with an ethical
question, stop. Take yourself out of the
situation. Think. Ask God for guidance (and
trust that He will provide it). Ask a
trustworthy adult whose life is patterned after
Jesus' what she would do in your place. And
read God's Word. No, you won't find a story
about a disciple struggling over what to do on
his math test hidden in the New Testament.
You won't find a Jewish girl trying to find her
best friend a date to the dance. But you will
find themes that readily apply to
your situation.

Lying, cheating, gossip, stealing, keeping promises, telling the truth—it's all in the Bible. Whatever your dilemma, it's likely that someone struggled with the same principle in biblical times. Tons of sticky situations that caused people to think twice about a question of right and wrong are recorded there. Though lots of people made mistakes that you won't want to follow, God's commands are clearly stated in His Word.

So, does the end ever justify the means? Sorry, I can't tell you. Ask God. Dig in. Pick up His Word and ask Him for insight. He will reveal to you His way. He will not fail you.

"No temptation has seized you except what is common to man. And God is faithful; he will not let you be tempted beyond what you can bear. But when you are tempted, he will also provide a way out so that you can stand up under it" (1 Corinthians 10:13).

Discover Your Destiny

The world's true movers and shakers share a secret—a common characteristic—that makes them stand out from the crowd: They are obsessed!

To be more specific, they are each compelled by *the magnificent obsession.*

That's right! Planet Earth's most successful people are each guided by a clear personal vision of what Christ wants them to accomplish in life. They've identified their talents and are using them to accomplish God's will. It may not be the type of success the world desires, but it's significant.

They are men and women of *destiny.*

Want less stress, more balance, and a more satisfying life? Of course you do. So, stop wasting your time and talent. Clue into God's will for your life and begin setting your true life goals.

Get a Clue—About God's Will

OK, let's get real: Figuring out God's will for your life is way too hard. It may even feel like some sort of mysterious riddle that's solved by only the holiest members of the Spiritual Elite Club.

But getting a clue about God's will doesn't have to be as hard as you think. It all boils down to *where* you look for answers and whom you listen to. It also involves staying in step with God.

Your life is filled with lots of simple situations that are easy to figure out—"baby step" situations (not choking your little brother when he annoys you or resisting the temptation to cheat on a test).

These kinds of circumstances require a basic knowledge of right and wrong. How do you get this sort of information? Let's explore some potential sources.

- **Television.** Bad choice. Learning right from wrong from the tube puts you in the "just tattoo 'Stupid' on my forehead and be done with it" category. Too much stuff beamed into your living room on TV goes against our Christian values and God's will for our lives. Also, keep in mind that many of the shows twist reality (in case you didn't notice, not everyone has perfect hair and teeth and a knockout bod).

- **Friends.** Fair choice, but you have to admit, your friends are walking beside you on the path—not ahead of you. So they probably don't have the kind of experience you need in order to know God's will. Of course, you shouldn't count them out completely. The Bible says there is wisdom in a multitude of counselors (see Proverbs 15:22). Sometimes, the advice of a good friend can help us make informed choices. Just be sure to choose your friends wisely.

- **Parents.** Good Choice. One of God's commandments is, "Obey and honor your parents." As you keep maturing, there are some decisions that your parents will want you to make on your own, like where you go to college, but others that they'll maintain the final word, like whether or not you can stay out all night with your friends. When it comes to making choices, it's very important that you hear them out, honor their direction, and obey when they give an absolute answer. If they make the wrong choice for you, God will deal with them and hold them accountable. You can rest assured that you've done the right thing by obeying.

  Obeying your parents now brings huge rewards later. It not only pleases God, who promises a blessing, but your parents will see you as a trustworthy and responsible daughter. This will pay off when they are willing to trust you to go and do things you really want to do.

  If, however, you don't obey them, then you will have the full responsibility for your decision on your own shoulders. You step out from under the umbrella of God's protection.

- **Bible.** Best choice. All Scripture is "God-breathed" and offers solid advice for just about every situation you'll ever encounter. Through the Word, God teaches, rebukes, corrects, and trains us in righteousness.

You'll hear all kinds of reasons why some people favor their feelings over the Bible: "It was written too long ago to really be relevant today." "It just doesn't make any sense to me." "No one can know for sure that it's 100 percent accurate."

Despite some people's doubts, God's Word IS timeless and absolutely, positively accurate in everything He knew was essential for us to know. That's far more trustworthy than our feelings, which change hour by hour. While there is room for debate on secondary issues (such as when the Rapture will occur), there are no discrepancies in God's promises, commands, and warnings. And the fact is, archaeologists and researchers are constantly making new discoveries that confirm the Bible's authority.

Beyond High School

Many girls go through high school with a survival mentality: *Survive my freshman year. Get past my sophomore year. Do well enough on the SAT and ACT to get into the college of my choice. Graduate.* While all that is good, it's a shortsighted way to live. You don't want to limit your view in college or later in your career. Don't forget that there's a far greater view you need to grab on to.

One day you will stand at the throne. "For we must all appear before the judgment seat of Christ, that each one may receive what is due him for the things done while in the body, whether good or bad" (2 Corinthians 5:10). If you're a believer, the question won't be heaven or hell. The question will be: How did you spend the life Jesus gave you? There's no way around it. You'll have to give an answer.

It's time to set some life goals with that day in mind. Goals for life have similarities to goals in sports. You strive to attain them. There's joy in achieving them. You long to execute them again. Yes. Goals are great.

Don't be afraid of setting some for your life.

Creating a Life Goal

There are three things you've got to remember about a life goal: It's concrete, measurable, and attainable.

A concrete goal is one you can put into words. A vague desire to "be a good Christian" is not very concrete. But "join InterVarsity Christian Fellowship my freshman year" is a solid goal. Goals are most concrete when written down.

A measurable goal is one that allows you to see progress. "Know the Bible from cover to cover" is tough to measure. But "read the New Testament this summer" allows you to mark your progress with that little ribbon dealie in your Bible.

An attainable goal is one that can reasonably be completed. "Lead the world to Christ" is both concrete and measurable, but hardly attainable. "Introduce three people to Jesus before I graduate from college" is a goal that meets all three criteria.

Once you have those three things, you can go for it.

Set Your Goals in Motion

Take an afternoon, a weekend, an hour a day for a month—whatever time you can—and pray. Above all, listen to God. Focus on His voice and direction for your life.

Also, begin working out the details by taking these simple steps:

- **Dare to dream.** No mouth-wide-open-snoring-on-the-pillow kind of stuff here. Think about your interests and desires. Consider the gifts and talents God has given you. Ask God to reveal what His good, pleasing, and perfect will should look like for you (Romans 12:2).

- **Plot a course.** Start writing some concrete, measurable, attainable goals for your life. Write a rough draft, then type them out. You'll want a clean copy to review and rehash on occasion in the future. Setting life goals shouldn't be a one-time affair.

- **Get some guidance.** Talk with your parents and/or an adult you trust who can possibly be your mentor. Let people know about your dreams and aspirations. Their input can be most valuable in finding the goals that will best shape the woman inside you.

And while you're at it, make this your overall target: When I've finished life's race, I want to hear Jesus say, "Well done" (Matthew 25:21). That's concrete. It's work, but it's measurable, and it's very attainable.

Get out of survival mode. Get proactive. Set some worthwhile life goals. And get ready for the Judgment Seat.

God's Power for You!

"Do you not know? Have you not heard? The LORD is the everlasting God, the Creator of the ends of the earth. He will not grow tired or weary, and his understanding no one can fathom. He gives strength to the weary and increases the power of the weak. Even youths grow tired and weary, and young men stumble and fall; but those who hope in the LORD will renew their strength. They will soar on wings like eagles; they will run and not grow weary, they will walk and not be faint."

—Isaiah 40:28-31

Part Five
Media Matters

A Dangerous Double Standard

"The most powerful nations are not those who have bombs, but those who control the media. That's where the battle is being fought; that is how you control people's minds."

—Filmmaker Spike Lee

Not all preachers stand in pulpits. Not all teachers shape minds in classrooms. And not everyone with something to sell does it in a 30-second commercial. With very little fanfare, entertainment communicates the beliefs and agendas of the people who create them. The screenwriter. The songwriter. The producer or director. And relatively few of them share a biblical worldview. Yet those messages really have an impact.

"Every study that I've ever seen that's done by the networks, the [movie] studios, educational organizations, tell us over and over again that we are all influenced by the media we consume," says Michael Warren, an executive producer at Warner Bros.

Of course, that's not *always* bad. Songs that celebrate peace, love, and strong family relationships can have a positive impact on the way people treat each other. Likewise, movies and TV shows often rally public sympathy and support for noble causes. But as members of the audience, we need to know when our buttons are being pushed. Although the entertainment industry hates to admit it, they don't always use their talents for our benefit.

Wheel of Fortune host Pat Sajak agrees that
show-biz people seem to race to take credit
for the *good* that comes from their work, but
are just as quick to distance themselves from
the bad. It's an age-old double standard. Sajak
said, "Television people have put blinders on,
and they absolutely refuse—and movie
people too—to admit that they can have any
influence for ill in our society. You know the
argument: 'We only reflect what's going on;
we don't perpetuate it.' And yet not a week
goes by in this town where there's not an
award ceremony where they're patting each
other on the back saying, 'You raised AIDS
awareness' [or] 'There'll be no more child
abuse thanks to that fine show you did.' The
argument is you can only influence for good;
you can't influence for ill. That makes no
sense at all."

For good or for ill, the media is persuasive.
Otherwise the TV network lucky enough to
air the Super Bowl each year wouldn't be able
to demand a record dollar amount for 30
seconds of air time. It may help to think of
the entertainment media the way you think
of fire or government. Neither isn't inherently
good or bad. Yet with fire, depending on
what it's used for and how it's handled, it can
either warm you and cook your food, or it
can burn your house to the ground. Media is
a powerful force that should be used
responsibly.

Fan Frenzy

It would be easy to bring up extreme cases of kids seeing films like *Scream* or *Jackass* and copying violent acts. We could spend pages (don't worry, we won't) detailing the crimes of people who made a habit of listening to hateful music and then went out and mimicked it. In fact, school shooter Jamie Rouse admitted to listening to Morbid Angel as a way of psyching himself up to murder a classmate ("It just made me feel capable of evil. It makes you feel like you want to kill someone"). From his prison cell Rouse said, "I used to think, 'This ain't affecting me. You'd have to be weak-minded to let this stuff affect you.' And the whole time it affected me—it helped shape the way I thought. . . . All those songs and the movies that make killing look cool. They don't show in the movies what it does to those people and their families. And sittin' in prison for the rest of your life isn't fun."

Clearly, Jamie Rouse and others like him are at the far end of the spectrum. But for every lover of violent entertainment who commits a crime or mimics a dumb stunt they saw on a big screen, countless others are being affected in a less visible way. They're being desensitized to suffering. Let's shift gears a second. In the sexual arena, will everyone who rents *American Pie* or watches *Friends* run out and have sex? Of course not. But a steady diet of immorality will make what's wrong seem right—or at least "normal." It can recondition our thinking and cause us to doubt the absolute standards spelled out in the Bible. And all because it's dismissed as harmless entertainment.

Media voices can undermine God's eternal truth and cause you to stumble. For example, you may have been taught that God's plan for sexuality is abstinence before marriage and faithfulness *afterward*. You've made that mental note. Yet popular entertainment promotes a very different attitude. The question isn't "Should I wait for marriage?" but rather "How long should we date before we do it?" Characters seem to have so much fun bouncing in and out of bed, especially since there are so few consequences in the land of make-believe. Then one day you get a pop quiz. Temptation comes knocking and you have to decide what's true, the spiritual standard you read in a book, or the one driven home time and time again by the amoral media with its airbrushed images and convincing gimmicks.

Colossians 2:8 warns, "See to it that no one takes you captive through hollow and deceptive philosophy, which depends on human tradition and the basic principles of this world rather than on Christ." No one is peddling more hollow and deceptive philosophy than the entertainment industry. And when worldly philosophies and morality masquerade as "fun," they can penetrate our hearts virtually unchallenged.

Cause and Effect

"[Violent entertainment's] effects are measurable and long-lasting."

—Part of a landmark joint statement by the American Medical Association, American Psychological Association, American Academy of Pediatrics, and American Academy of Child and Adolescent Psychiatry on the impact of violent entertainment on youth

Blooming Among the Weeds

"...The Lord has assigned to each his task. I planted the seed, Apollos watered it, but God made it grow."

—1 Corinthians 3:5-6

In his first letter to the Corinthian church, the apostle Paul alluded to the way God's Word is spread and nurtured. He used a simple farming metaphor to make his point: Paul sowed. Apollos watered. Each played an important part in the grand plan of growth. As we know from Jesus' parable of the sower in Luke 8, plants rarely flourish without some opposition. Like thorns. Or *weeds*. We could classify "weeds" as pretty much *anything* that could entangle our spirit and interfere with growth.

Okay, back to sowing and watering for a second. Your parents—as well as your pastor—may be sowing God's Word into your life in a powerful way. And it's getting watered every week at youth group. So far so good. *Now what about the weeds?* Make no mistake, they're there. What most teen girls fail to realize is that "weeds" in the form of unhealthy entertainment can spring up and choke out holiness. That includes explicit stuff, but also subtle messages that can be even *more* damaging. We've already pointed out the power of media messages. Now is the hard part: While others can sow and water your life, only *you* can take care of the weeds.

Walking with Jesus Christ requires "discernment." Discernment is just a fancy term for the kind of wisdom that helps us choose between right and wrong, good and bad. You're faced with decisions constantly. Wouldn't it be cool to know you're making the right ones? King Solomon thought so. In fact, he valued discernment so much that when God said he could have anything he wanted, Solomon asked for discernment (wisdom) *instead* of money or a long life (1 Kings 3).

Spiritual insight starts with the Bible. God's Word gives us a yardstick for measuring all kinds of things—from music lyrics to video games—to see if they meet His standards. Sometimes a video box or CD cover says it all. Other times it's less obvious.

Want to be like Jesus? Then pray for discernment and ask God to give you His mind concerning popular culture.

"My son, preserve sound judgment and discernment, do not let them out of your sight."

—King Solomon in Proverbs 3:21

The Battle Within

It's important to remember that there's a battle going on inside your heart. Galatians 5:17 explains, "For the sinful nature desires what is contrary to the Spirit, and the Spirit what is contrary to the sinful nature. They are in conflict with each other, so that you do not do what you want." Do you know that feeling? Have you ever flipped through *Cosmo Girl* at a magazine rack? Did you wonder if maybe you'd get a lot more attention in one of those micro-miniskirts or if you could brag about the latest gossip on a certain celebrity? C'mon, admit it. *Cosmo* knows what tempts you. The filmmakers behind the teen flicks know it. Everyone gets tempted, but with God's help we don't have to give in to it.

The flesh and spirit hunger for different things. The flesh has an appetite for "junk food." That could include anything from crude sitcoms and sexually suggestive music, to romance novels, to magazines that peddle fragrances and fashions that glorify lust and carnal behavior. The spirit, on the other hand, feeds on studying the Bible, praying, redemptive themes, godly input, and service to others (Romans 13:14 encourages "spirit-fed" living; Galatians 5:22 details the benefits). A lot of entertainment and advertising panders to the flesh: lust, greed, vengeance, jealousy. The more you *feed* that inherent nature, the more it will come from your life and heart.

A lot of teens make the mistake of "compart-mentalizing" their Christian faith. In other words, an intimate walk with the Lord only applies to certain areas of their lives. Not good enough. Jesus wants to be Lord of *all*. Consider Him when you buy a movie ticket. Don't shut Him out when you put on a set of headphones or when you pick up a magazine. Think critically about entertainment.

"Beware of going to the funeral of your own independence. The natural life is not spiritual and it can only be made spiritual by sacrifice. We go wrong because we stubbornly refuse to discipline ourselves, physically, morally or mentally. Our natural life must not rule; God must rule in us."

—Oswald Chambers, author of
My Utmost for His Highest

Are There Boundaries?

It's difficult to know what's in bounds and what's out of bounds if we base decisions on box-office numbers, record sales, ratings, or what our friends think. Isn't there anything more reliable and absolute? You bet there is! The Bible includes lots of verses that apply, even though it was written centuries before Buffy started slaying vampires. But maybe the true test for entertainment should be 2 Peter 1:5-8.

The author says, "Make every effort to add to your faith goodness; and to goodness, knowledge; and to knowledge, self-control; and to self-control, perseverance; and to perseverance, godliness; and to godliness, brotherly kindness; and to brotherly kindness, love. For if you possess these qualities in increasing measure, they will keep you from being ineffective and unproductive in your knowledge of our Lord Jesus Christ." Are you possessing those qualities "in increasing measure"? If not, maybe it's because so much of today's entertainment devalues things like godliness, self-control, and brotherly kindness.

Make choices that *reinforce* the positive. That means eliminating messages that undermine your Christlike character.

"Test everything. Hold on to the good. Avoid every kind of evil."
—1 Thessalonians 5:21-22

Of course, when you draw your moral line between right and wrong, someone is bound to disagree. "What about " 'Don't judge lest you be judged!' " they say as they wag a finger in your face. The fact is that in this verse Jesus is warning against judging others' thoughts, motives, and the *hidden* things of the heart. Jesus is not talking about ignoring sin or refusing to make moral judgments and practice discernment. When the evidence is there, it's our responsibility to make wise judgments on our quest for holiness.

Music and
the Message

"There is nothing more singular about this generation than its addiction to music."

—Allan Bloom in his best-selling book,
The Closing of the American Mind

Believe it or not, that statement was written in 1987. Yet it's as true today as ever. Your friends—maybe even you—spend an amazing amount of time listening to music. The average teen hears 10,500 hours of music between grades 7 and 12. That equals more than 14 months of nonstop tunage. And it's not just listening to the radio; it's also CDs. In 1999, the music industry sold a record 754.8 million albums. And that's not just boy bands either. Rap. Rock. Country. Hip-hop. Pop. Christian. What do those songs *say?* And why does it matter?

The Power of Music —It's All in Your Head

Ever thought about how easy it is to get a tune stuck in your head? You only need to hear a few bars and—*zap!*—it's buzzing around in there for hours. And often, it's not just the music. The words rattle around in there too. Music travels with us, for good or bad, tending to go in one ear and out the other.

Or *does* it?

Catchy melodies have a way of grabbing something in our subconscious and hitching a ride. They hook you without much warning and sometimes you have to shake them loose. Ever tried to get a particularly repetitive song out of your head? What do you have to do? Sing a different song, right?

Billboard magazine ran a guest commentary by Dr. Richard Pellegrino, a brain specialist with a fascinating take on the power of music. He talked about potent chemical reactions in the brain. He explained how music can actually improve visual and spatial reasoning, memory, and learning. After discussing "music's immense power" and urging artists and producers to use that power wisely, Dr. Pellegrino concluded, "Take it from a brain guy: In 25 years of working with the human brain, I still cannot affect a person's state of mind the way that one simple song can."

"We've put out songs with lyrics in them that we thought people would think were funny, but they ended up having a lot of really negative effects on people. [Performers] need to be aware that when you're creating music it has a tremendous influence on society."

—Adam Youch of Beastie Boys

Explicit Stuff

Lyrics about sex and drugs aren't new. Sure, they've gotten bolder since your parents were in high school, but even back then some music strayed out of bounds. In the late 1970s, Eric Clapton had a hit single titled "Cocaine." And while oldies might not use graphic sexual slang, songs like Billy Joel's "Only the Good Die Young" and Meat Loaf's "Paradise by the Dashboard Light" still had their hormones in overdrive.

Joel now admits that people who raised concerns about early rock music had a valid point. "All those things they were saying about rock 'n' roll in the early days—'Oh, it's gonna subvert our youth. It's gonna make 'em all want to have sex. It's gonna make 'em all go crazy'—they were *right*." Quite a confession. Today, chart-topping lyrics continue to get more and more explicit, making the need for discernment even more crucial.

"Music is such a powerful medium now. The kids don't even know who the president is, but they know what's on MTV. I think if anyone like Hitler or Mussolini were alive now, they would have to be rock stars."

—Marilyn Manson

Music is a mighty motivator—even when it's not trying to be. Def Jam Records founder Russel Simmons was quite proud when Jay-Z's casual reference to a clothing company inspired a run on designer sweaters. "Jay-Z raps about Iceberg and it catches fire," Simmons boasted. "That's a fact. The minute he said it, Saks Fifth Avenue blows out Iceberg sweaters at what?—$600 apiece. Instantly!" And what of Jay-Z's lyrics that make illicit sex, gang violence, and drunk driving look cool? Are we to believe they have absolutely *no* impact whatsoever? If they're honest, even the artists don't really believe that. It seems more and more musicians are rethinking choices they've made, including goth-rocker Trent Reznor of Nine Inch Nails who said, "I think *The Downward Spiral* actually could be harmful through implying and subliminally suggesting things."

Perform Surgery

Okay, so the messages in songs have a powerful impact. So what? What's a young woman of God supposed to do to be discerning and defend herself?

Start by *dissecting and discarding*.

It's like in biology where you cut up the frog. You take out your spiritual scalpel and start into a song to take a closer look at its insides. What do the lyrics really say? When you dissect a frog, you use a chart to tell you what to look for and what that particular part does. It's the same as when dissecting a song. You can use the truth of Scripture as a guide to see what you're dealing with. Does a disc include profanity? Proverbs 4:24 says, "Put away perversity from your mouth; keep corrupt talk far from your lips." Does it present promiscuous women as attractive role models? Proverbs 24:1 warns, "Do not envy wicked men [or women], do not desire their company." Does it advocate hatred or disrespect toward Mom and Dad? Exodus 20:12 tells us to *honor* our parents.

More than a scalpel, the Word of God is a double-edged sword (Hebrews 4:12) with an answer for everything. Those verses and others will help you skillfully *dissect* song lyrics. Then, once you've done that, it's time to discard anything that contradicts God's healthy plan for your life. It's never easy to say "adios" to favorite CDs that don't make the cut. Just keep in mind that purifying your music library is essential if you're serious about achieving personal holiness.

Christian Record Labels

Essential Records
www.EssentialRecords.com
(Caedmon's Call, FFH, Jars of Clay)

Fervent Records
www.FerventRecords.com
(Big Daddy Weave, By The Tree)

Forefront Records
www.ForefrontRecords.com
(DC Talk, Rebecca St. James)

Inotof Records
www.Inotof.com
(Sara Groves, SonicFlood, Mercy Me)

Integrity Music
www.IntegrityMusic.com
(Darrel Evans, Hillsong, Hosanna! Music)

Reunion Records
www.ReunionRecords.com
(Michael W. Smith, Joy Williams)

Rocketown Records
www.RocketownRecords.com
(Ginny Owens, Chris Rice)

Sparrow Records
www.SparrowRecords.com
(Andy Hunter, Avalon, Newsboys)

Word Records
www.WordRecords.com

Ardent Records
www.ArdentRecords.com
(Todd Agnew [rock/jazz], Justifide)

FlickerRecords.com
www.FlickerRecords.com
(Pillar, Royal Ruckus [hip-hop])

Gotee Records
www.Gotee.com
(GRITS [hip-hop], Jennifer Knapp)

Inpop Records
www.Inpop.com
(Phil Joel, Superchic[k])

Metro 1 Music
www.Metro1Music.com
(Juggernautz, Crystal Lewis, Michael Knott)

Forty Records
www.40Records.com

Lion of Zion Entertainment
www.LionofZion.com

Solid State Records
www.SolidStateRecords.com

Rhythm House Records
www.RhythmHouse.com

Silent Planet Records
www.SilentPlanetRecords.com

Verity Records
www.verityrecordsonline.com

—Compiled by Loren Eaton.
Focus on the Family does not endorse any of these
record companies. This list is for reference only.

Your Brain, the Box Office, and You

"Film is a powerful medium. Film is a drug. Film is a potential hallucinogen. It goes into your eye. It goes into your brain. It stimulates. And it's a dangerous thing. It can be a very subversive thing."

—Oliver Stone, director of *Platoon*, *JFK*, and *Natural Born Killers*

A dark theater. Reclining seats. Surround sound. Hot-buttered popcorn. There's something almost magical about seeing a movie on the big screen. Add friends and a cold drink to the mix and you've got the makings of a perfect afternoon, right? Not so fast. There's more to a motion picture than cool special effects and a rip-roaring soundtrack. The images and messages contained in films can leave a permanent mark on our attitudes—whether we want them to or not.

"Two girls came up to me and said they'd changed their names on their birth certificates to Sarah, so they could be just like my character on Party of Five.*"*

—Jennifer Love Hewitt

Until 1995, the residents of Fiji couldn't watch television. It simply didn't exist there. Immediately after it was introduced, the islanders noticed a sharp rise in eating disorders. Then, just three years after TV, 74 percent of girls said they felt "too big or too fat."

"Nobody was dieting in Fiji ten years ago," reports Harvard Medical School anthropology professor Anne Becker. "The teenagers see TV as a model for how one gets by in the modern world. They believe the shows depict reality."

Is it much different in North America? From fashions to hairstyles, we take many of our cues from what we see on the big screen or on the tube. Our "reality" is shaped by it. And it's not just the way we look. Often it's the way we talk. The way we think. The way we act.

Movies featuring explicit sex, violence, language, or the occult are no-brainers. They're clearly out of bounds based on verses such as Philippians 4:8, Colossians 2:8, Psalm 101:3, and 1 John 2:15-17. However, some movies can be a lot of fun! The important thing is that you don't leave your brains in the lobby after the dude in the vest tears your ticket. Here are just a few questions to ask as you watch movies:

- "What's the point?" Boil the flick down to its most basic theme. What's it trying to say?

- "Which characters am I being asked to root for? Are they virtuous people, or am I supposed to find immorality heroic?"

- "Are the characters thinking about the long-term consequences of their decisions? If I went out and did the stuff the people onscreen are doing, what would probably happen in the real world?"

- "What is the filmmaker trying to get me to think or feel? Would that enrich my spiritual life or could it drag me down?"

- *Identify the "power source."* "Where do the characters find strength and answers to their problems? Is it in God and eternal truth, or do they rely on human wisdom or the occult to deal with conflict? What does the story say about God?"

"Half the business called Hollywood is sleaze. A lot of what we do has very little to do with art. It has to do with sleaze and gratuitous sex and unnecessary violence."

—Film and television actor Martin Sheen

When to Take a Stand

Have you ever been sitting there munching your Raisinettes and out of nowhere came an explicit sex scene, some brutal violence, or a really raunchy joke? What did you do? Most girls would brush it off and keep watching. After all, who drops 10 bucks on admission and snacks and then walks out after only 15 minutes? Frankly, *a woman of God!* The Lord cares deeply about the stuff we put into our systems. If we're serious about following Him, we need to be more concerned about our spiritual fitness than about how much money we spent or what our friends might think. (By the way, most theater managers will give you a refund or a comp ticket if you skip out on a film because of offensive content.)

Teens who have taken that kind of stand are leaders. They're bold. They want to do what's right regardless of the cost. Romans 12:1(NASB) says we must present ourselves to God as "a living and holy sacrifice."

There's a cost involved. If you go out and buy designer clothes, you pay a price to wear that designer's name. On your chest. On your back pocket. On your hat. Your shoes. The cost depends on the designer. Well, if you want to bear the name of Jesus, there's a similar cost involved. But it's not a one-time charge of $90 for a pair of jeans or a blouse. It's a price we pay every day in the choices we make.

Know Before You Go

If you don't like the idea of walking out on a movie (who does?), there are ways to avoid getting into that situation in the first place. Learn as much as you can about a movie *before* heading to the local cineplex. Web sites like pluggedinmag.com or previewonline.org can give you the scoop on new movies from a Christian perspective so you'll know what's in store. If, after doing a little research, you and your parents agree that it's an okay flick, go for it! If you see something that you don't believe God would consider appropriate, listen to the Holy Spirit's leading.

Sometimes it's real tempting to go along with the crowd when a bunch of friends are dead-set on checking out a certain film. Yet you know it's not right. What do you do? Without being judgmental, let them know you'd rather not see the movie, but you can meet up afterward at the mall or some other place. This reinforces that you're *most* interested in spending time with your friends—not sitting in a dark theater where you can't even talk to each other. Don't make them think you're judging them for going to the movie. It's your moral stand you're taking, not theirs. Then, if the Holy Spirit chooses to convict someone through the stand you're taking, you can't be held responsible.

What About R-rated?

"Can I watch an R-rated movie and still be a Christian?" That question deserves a closer look.

First things first. Watching an R-rated movie doesn't make anyone a sinner in and of itself. The question itself reveals a fundamental misunderstanding of what it really means to be a Christian. *Salvation* has nothing to do with your entertainment choices. That's set. You're a Christian because you believe in what Jesus did on the cross. It's a gift you can't earn or deserve. Asking, "Can I watch an R-rated movie and still be a Christian?" makes two false assumptions: that going to an R-rated movie is inherently un-Christian, and that relationship with God is based on what we do—works. Remember, you bear the name "Christian" because of what Jesus did, not what you do.

Yes, we should avoid entertainment God would disapprove of. And R-rated movies warn that they include some pretty offensive stuff. Whether or not the good in a film outweighs the bad is often a decision only the Holy Spirit can make. If you feel that twinge of conscience, better skip it. But don't skip any movie out of fear that if you see it you'll lose your place in heaven. Rather, say no in response to what Jesus did for you on the cross, out of love for Him. He paid the price for you. If you intend to serve Him—and want His best for your life—strive to honor Him in everything you do. That includes the movies you check out, both at the theater and on video.

What's on the Tube?

"I know I'm biting the hand that feeds me, but TV can really suck the brains right out of your body."

—Kristen Johnson of the NBC sitcom *3rd Rock from the Sun*

It's kind of funny when you stop to think about it. The same average people who say television has no power at all will go to wild extremes to be *seen* on it. They appear on humiliating talk shows like *Jerry Springer* and risk embarrassment on reality series like *Survivor* or *Road Rules*. Everyone knows that TV gets seen and has the ability to impact viewers. But no one seems as quick to admit that it may skew your view.

Don't Let TV Skew Your View

Television sends out a constant stream of messages on what seem like 40 million channels. An awful lot of those messages sell you and your friends the wrong impressions about sex (and other things). Suggestive advertising. Racy music videos. Salacious news items. And what about shows like *Friends* and *Dawson's Creek* that make sex outside of marriage—even homosexuality—seem normal and enticing?

A while back, *YM* magazine published the results of an online poll of nearly 15,000 teenage girls. It asked them why they were choosing to have sex. As it turned out, the number-one reason girls decided to become sexually active was *curiosity*. More than half (58%) said they gave away their most intimate gift because they wondered what all the fuss was about.

What fuels that kind of curiosity? Well, one thing we know is that sitcom humor is *obsessed* with sex. TV dramas often use sexuality to spice up subplots. A year-long study of the WWF's "Raw Is War" by folks at Indiana University found 128 simulated sex acts in and around the ring. And the worst of the worst? MTV. From videos to reality shows to pseudo game shows, sex is referenced an unbelievable number of times per hour. With sex getting so much attention on the tube, is it any wonder so many teens get curious?

What could all those shows be so obsessed about anyway?

Take Every Thought Captive

Despite never seeing HBO, the apostle Paul knew how effectively Satan uses our idle thoughts against us. That's why he warned the Corinthian church, "Take every thought captive to make it obedient to Christ" (2 Corinthians 10:5). Think of that next time you're channel surfing. For the serious-minded woman of God, there's no such thing as "vegging out with mindless TV." You've got to stay sharp.

"You can bury my TV. There's nothing to watch—just bad things and naked people."

—An elderly Moscow woman after an antenna fire disrupted TV broadcasting there

Keep Your Brain Engaged

Soaking up sexual images and philosophies is just one prime-time hazard for girls. There are others. Some shows can inspire an unhealthy fascination with the occult. Some rely heavily on violence. The point is, TV shows reflect the worldviews of the people making them. And how often do you see that being a biblical worldview? A woman of God has to keep her brain engaged at all times. Here are some things to think about:

- **In a sitcom, "problems" are introduced and solved in under 30 minutes.** As you may have noticed, real life rarely works that way.

- **When you see a scene of violence or emotional cruelty on a show or in a commercial, is the perpetrator punished?** Are you led to empathize with the victim's suffering, or is their pain simply meant to entertain you? Avoid being desensitized.

- **On television, there's a great deal of emphasis on people's looks.** The female leads are a relatively selective group: size two body, perfect hair, pearly white smile. Remember the words of 1 Samuel 16:7, "The LORD does not look at the things man looks at. Man looks at the outward appearance, but the LORD looks at the heart."

- **TV often relies on stereotypes.** For example, in a 30-minute show, it's faster and easier to portray a "nerdy girl" by making her a total klutz with bad skin, clothes, and buck teeth than to develop her as a normal human being. Don't let the TV shortcuts affect the way you view people.

- **Plan your viewing ahead of time.** It's easy to channel surf an afternoon away without ever resting on a show for more than five minutes at a time. Grab a highlighter and the TV Guide. Then budget a realistic amount of time each week for the tube and make wise choices.

- **Sometimes the best course of action is to turn off the set.** Prime-time companionship can't compare to hours spent with godly friends. The apostle Paul told young Timothy, "Flee the evil desires of youth, and pursue righteousness, faith, love and peace, along with those who call on the Lord out of a pure heart" (2 Timothy. 2:22).

A Web of Choices

So you like sailing through cyberspace? Saving the planet from rogue aliens? Editing your own movies? Computer technology moves faster all the time, but if anybody moves just as fast, it's teen girls. Can you even remember when there wasn't an Internet?

Yet, as with other aspects of life, the virtual world has a good side . . . and a dark side. Many girls are using the Web for positive—even eternal—purposes. Unfortunately, girls (not to mention thousands of other teens and adults—even *Brio* readers) are logging on to the bad stuff, too.

So what are all those teens logging on to? Take a look:

Bulletin boards. Chat rooms. Photo galleries. Video viewing rooms. Music downloads. Encyclopedias. Entire libraries of info. There are plenty of good reasons to cruise cyberspace. Log on to the Web, click the mouse, and you're walking the halls of the U.S. Capitol. *Click* again and you're face-to-face with a pride of lions on an African safari. *Click.* A NASA Web page—with tons of information that'll help you with your big report. *Click.* A Bible story. *Click.* Encode. *Click.* You can create a homepage for your own youth group.

Anarchist ideologies. *Click.* Drug connections. *Click.* The occult. *Click.* Sexual predators. *Click.* Digital piracy.

Click. Click. Click. You started in your best friend's video game review site and within a few quick clicks ended up in archives of hard-core pornography. *Click.* Gambling site with no hint of the big-time financial ruin behind its glittery facade.

According to the Pew Internet & American Life Project, 94 percent of teens online report researching on the Internet for school projects.

Nearly 60 percent of teens have received an IM or e-mail from a stranger.

15 percent of online teens have lied about their age to access a Web site—an act often used to enter a pornographic site.

Our technologically driven society *demands* a working knowledge of "virtual" interaction. Much of the academic and business worlds are totally dependent on this far-reaching technology for research, information, and countless other activities. Thousands trade stocks and bank online. Public libraries, churches, and schools have launched Web sites. And Christian ministries that spread the gospel get a lot of help from the mass communication inherent to the Internet.

Obviously, pulling the plug on cyberspace isn't so easy in this day and age. So what to do? How can you get the good stuff . . . and avoid the bad?

About 17 million teens and [preteens] ages 12 to 17 use the Internet (73%).

Navigation Tips

It all begins with a pretty simple, time-honored concept—watch where you wander. Or, in this case, watch where you click.

The Web is like a big city whose real estate is cheap and therefore easy to snatch up for whatever you want to build. It's an amazing megalopolis of cyber-circuitry with wide boulevards and narrow alleys, churches next to night clubs and child sites next to casinos. It also contains an overflowing cyber-sewer and a red-light district of sleazy bookstores and smut shops. But remember, when Jesus promised his assistance and companionship, *"to the very end of the age"* (Matthew 28:20), He *already* knew all about the Internet. His power and friendship stretch into cyberspace too.

Okay, we know what you're thinking: *It can't actually hurt you. It's just a Web site. You can always just turn off the computer.*

True. But teen girls can get hurt—and have—in that vast emptiness of digitized danger that's just a click away. Fortunately, cruising safely down the information superhighway is possible. You've just got to use some biblical standards and old-fashioned common sense.

Try these tested tips for getting a grip on the information superhighway:

Cut off the source. Many filtering software packages block sexually explicit material before it gets to your screen. Get one. Don't surf alone. Stay off the Web when you're home alone. You never know what or who is going to find you surfing around and want to "talk."

Stick to wide open spaces. Keep the computer out of your bedroom and in a common area, like the kitchen or den.

Keep accountable. Surfing with a close friend or a parent encourages you to monitor your time online.

Don't use the computer after the rest of your family is in bed. Just like city streets, the Internet (especially chat rooms) is more hazardous when traversed in the dark.

Be street smart. This is especially true in cyberspace: Don't talk to strangers.

Guard your family's privacy. Never give out your name, address, phone number, or any other personal information on the Web.

Don't chat alone. IM a friend and take her along. You can carry on your own conversations but know that a bud can back you up—and keep you from posing as that 21-year-old, Ferrari-driving swimsuit model.

Leave chat rooms immediately if anyone ever pressures you to talk, harasses you in any way, or asks for personal information. Never respond to suggestive, belligerent, sexual, abusive, or degrading messages. Always let your service provider know if these things happen to you.

Never go alone to meet anyone face-to-face. If you do discover someone on the Net you want to hook up with in the real world, make sure your parents are with you and make sure the meeting happens in a public place.

Never play with pornographic sites. Satan will try to tell you otherwise, but the sites are dangerous. For the same reason you would never play with matches in a closet, you should never, ever visit sordid Web sites.

Good Web Sites

Brio Get what's in print (and more) on your screen: www.BrioMag.com

Plugged In Music and movie reviews: www.pluggedinmag.com

"Life on the Edge Live!" Live talk radio show for and with teens: www.family.org/lote/lotelive

Boundless.org Webzine for college students.

Christian Teens Info and links on issues, faith, missions, and more: www.christianteens.about.com

Encarta Encyclopedia site includes homework help: www.encarta.msn.com Encyclopedia.com

ChristianStudents.com

Made4More.com Questions and answers about life, sex, and hope.

Musicforce.com The latest Christian CDs.

Petersons.com Comprehensive guide to colleges, career planning, even summer camps and programs.

Reference: Best Source for Facts on the Net You name it, this site's got it: facts, info, trivia, news, maps, etc.: www.refdesk.com

See You at the Pole All about the event, the ministry, and more: www.syatp.com

CCMMagazine.com Latest inside Christian music.

Sports Spectrum Christian sports magazine. www.sport.org

Part Six
Money Matters

Success in God's Eyes

Pick up any dictionary and it might define success like this: "1: a favorable result. 2: the attainment of wealth, favor, or eminence." That's what success is, but what does it mean to be *successful?*

You could say that a person who is successful is someone who sets lots of goals and then continually achieves them. But that's not exactly what most people think of when they say someone is a success.

If a person is considered successful, she's probably at the top of her career. Who's the most famous super model right now? That person is probably a success in the world's book. And what about the most popular actress, pulling down the top salary, and starring in the best movies? To most people that woman is a success.

At this point in your life you probably haven't narrowed down exactly what you want to be when you become an adult. However, if you land at the top of your career, if you're totally rich and look fabulous, will you be successful?

According to Barna Research Online (www.barna.org):

- 51 percent of Christians and 54 percent of non-Christians believe that money is the main symbol of success in life.

- 32 percent of Christians and 44 percent of non-Christians say money is very important to them.

- 19 percent of Christians and 20 percent of non-Christians feel like you can tell how successful someone is by looking at what they own.

It's important to understand that God sees success differently from the world. He doesn't look at how many magazine covers a person is on or how much money she brings home from commercial endorsements. God doesn't care what kind of car a person drives, how big her house is, or even if she owns a platinum credit card with no spending limit. All the power, money, and fame in the world doesn't impress God in the slightest.

So how does God define success? To begin, look at a few of the biblical characters who were successful in His eyes:

- Esther—She became queen of Persia, a place where women didn't have a lot of power or freedom. But Esther used her beauty, brains, and faith to save her people from annihilation at the hands of wicked Haman.

- Joseph—As a teen he dreamed of becoming the ruler of a nation. After being sold into slavery by his own brothers, and spending years rotting in a jail, God moved him from the dungeon to Egypt's governor's palace overnight!

- David—As a young shepherd and the youngest member of his family, David tended the family's flocks. While he watched the sheep he developed a passionate faith in the Almighty. As a result, God made David the king of Israel!

- Deborah—A judge and a prophetess, Deborah was a respected leader in Israel. She inspired Barak to obey God and led Israel into a victorious battle against Sisera.

- Tabitha—Also known as Dorcas, Tabitha lived in Joppa, a coastal city where many men died at sea, leaving behind destitute wives and children. Tabitha was a skilled seamstress who made clothes for the widows and orphans of her city and gave generously to help them. She was so well loved that when she died, her friends sent for Peter, who raised her from the dead.

When we look at this list we see that the common denominator is faith. These people all had a deep, unshakable, loving, and transforming faith in God. A faith like that doesn't just happen overnight. It comes as a result of building a powerful relationship with God over a long period of time.

Success in God's eyes is how much we love Him and desire to serve Him. A girl whose faith leads to godly success

- **asks,** "God, is this what You want?"

- **says,** "I'll do Your will, God."

- **looks** to satisfy God's wishes.

- **seeks** not man's approval but God's.

- **measures** success not by how well things are going, but by how well her life is centered in God's will.

- **respects** herself greatly, and still puts her needs behind others.

- **solves** problems by relying on God's power, not her abilities alone.

Success in God's eyes means a person must be willing to give up everything—her self, her possessions, her pride, her power—in order to gain what God has in store. It's sometimes true that in doing so, a woman may never achieve what she dreamed she'd always become. However, more times than not, when a person fully surrenders her life, God returns those dreams and talents. And one thing is always true: God's plans for you are bigger, grander, and wilder than you could ever imagine.

Bottom line, if you want to become a success in God's eyes, choose to surrender everything to God and His will for your life.

Your 10 Percent

So are you fully surrendered to God? Are you totally trusting Him to provide your needs on a daily basis? What about your finances? Does God have control of those too? God asks us to give back from what He has blessed us with.

Some people say tithing was an Old Testament principle. And it's true that when Jesus came, Christians were "no longer under the law, but under grace." Yet nowhere in the New Testament does it say that Christians *shouldn't* give. And at the very least, tithing is a good principle for Christians to live by. We should want to give back to God for His many blessings. And one of those ways of giving back is to tithe.

- Tithe is an Old English word that simply means "tenth."

- God asked Israel to return 10 percent of their moneys.

- God promised to pour out blessings on those who tithe.

- God challenged Israel to see if He wouldn't bless them more for tithing.

In our consumer society, one of the most difficult areas to put under God's control is our money. Having total control of one's finances is a way to demonstrate a person's success to the world. There's not always a visible return on tithing to God's kingdom. It's hard to see the point.

Yet if you're on God's pathway to success, your finances will be also. In fact, if you trust Him completely in this area, He's promised to flood your life with uncountable blessings.

Tithing Your Time

OK, we've discussed tithing your money, but what about your time? Isn't tithing our money enough? What else could God want?

Though the Bible never actually says it, tithing of your time is good stewardship. Jesus told His disciples that time spent serving others wasn't just something they should do; it was a priority. Throughout the Gospels, Jesus demonstrated this. He healed the sick, fed multitudes, cast out demons, and touched broken hearts. He met the needs of those He came in contact with and He hoped the Church would do the same.

Think of your community, your family, your school, your church, and the wider world. How have you invested in serving the hungry, teaching the illiterate, visiting the sick and elderly, or helping the poor? If you can't think of anything, try praying about it and ask God to show you where you might be able to begin.

Remember God's definition of a success? It includes putting others first. If you want to be successful in God's eyes, serving others is important. And tithing your time to God is a great way to start.

What Jesus Said About Serving

- If anyone wants to be first, he must be last, the servant of all (see Mark 9:35).

- Whoever wants to become great must be a servant (see Mark 10:43-45).

- The greatest should be like the youngest, and the one who rules like the one who serves (see Luke 22:26-27).

- Blessed are the merciful, for they will be shown mercy (see Matthew 5:7).

Green-Eyed Greed

Let's review. Success in God's eyes has nothing to do with how much you make or achieve. Success in God's eyes comes from total submission to His purpose and plan for your life. To be a success in God's eyes, you must be willing to lose everything for the cause of Christ.

An easy way to kill godly success is to let greed enter your life. That's right. Greed.

Greed is the overwhelming desire for money, power, and possessions. Greed is always self-centered and it can never be satisfied. It always wants more and does not care how it gets it. Greed destroys lives.

In Mark 10, Jesus was approached by a rich young man. He asked what he had to do to receive eternal life and Jesus told him to "Go, sell everything you have and give to the poor, and you will have treasure in heaven. Then come, follow me" (v. 21). The young man's face fell. The price was too high. He couldn't give up his possessions.

Understand that Jesus wasn't asking the man to become a pauper or to give away everything. He was asking him to forfeit his opulent lifestyle. The young man was rich, but inside he was empty. He'd become greedy.

After the young man left, Jesus looked at his disciples and said, "It is easier for a camel to go through the eye of a needle than for a rich man to enter the kingdom of God" (10:25). In God's eyes, it's simple. When a person is greedy, she doesn't give a rip about what God wants, and as a result, she has no part in God's kingdom.

So if you ever catch yourself flirting with greedy thoughts, stop and ask forgiveness. Ask God to change your heart by removing any nuggets of greed and replacing them with seeds of humility and self-sacrifice.

God's Will Is...

- self-sacrifice
- to always put others first
- to give to the work of His kingdom
- for you to help the needy

Greed's Will Is...

- self-gratification
- to use others for personal gain
- to keep everything for yourself
- for you to help yourself

Dollars and Sense

Get this: According to Teen Research Unlimited (www.teenresearch.com), in the year 2000, American teenagers spent more than $155 billion. *Yikes!*

On average, most teens spent about $84 per week. More than two-thirds of that is earned on their own. About a third—$27—is their parents' money. Some financial analysts believe that the $155 billion figure could increase by 20 or 30 percent over the next five years. That's a lot of cash floating around—all controlled by teenagers.

Because you represent a huge portion of the market, retailers pay advertisers lots of money to convince you to buy their products. It's the advertisers' job. They don't want you keeping your money. And they'll stop at nothing to make you think you should throw your hard-earned cash in their direction.

Historically, they've been pretty convincing. Like thousands of other teens, you've probably seen an advertisement and thought, *I just gotta have that!* After you bought it, how long did you use it? Did you buy on a whim? Maybe you don't spend anywhere near the average $84, but if you were to save half— $42 a week—at the end of a year you'd have $2,184. If you started doing this at age 12, by the time you turned 16 you'd have almost $9,000. Add 4 percent interest: that's nearly $10,000.

What Is Stewardship?

A *steward* is defined as one who manages another's property, finances, or affairs. *Stewardship* refers to how a person handles herself in a particular job.

From a biblical perspective, God is the owner of all that exists, providing us with all our needs. We are *stewards* of what He gives and stewardship is how we handle His resources. If we look at the way Jesus taught and the things He said, good stewardship is the overwhelming theme that comes through. He often taught by telling stories to illustrate an important point. Of the more than 30 parables Jesus told, about half of them included lessons in different aspects of stewardship.

In Luke 15:11-32, Jesus shares one of his most famous parables, the Prodigal Son: A man's youngest son walks in and says, "Dad, I don't think I want to wait until you're dead. I'd like my inheritance now if you don't mind." So the dad gives him a big load of cash and watches him scamper off to a faraway country to go hog-wild. He blows the money on partying and winds up completely broke. The only way he can survive is to take a job with a local pig farmer. Eventually, he looks around and realizes the servants in his father's house live way better. He decides he'll just go home and beg his father to let him be a servant.

When his father sees him coming, he's so excited that he runs out to meet him, kissing and hugging him. He says, "Get this boy a bath, my finest suit, and go prepare a feast. Tonight we celebrate my son's return!" Jesus' story illustrates the mercy and grace God extends when we blow it. That's the main point, but there's another great lesson in there on how God views our self-indulgence.

Miss everything else, but don't miss this: The father in this story owned all the wealth. He gives it to the youngest son who goes off to squander it. He doesn't even invest! And when he's completely bankrupt, eating pig slop, and smelling like a barn, he realizes just how wrong he's been. And that's when he's finally learned what a *steward* is.

One of the reasons God blesses us is so we'll learn to be good stewards. When we waste it on useless stuff, we're living outside with the pigs. As in the parable of the prodigal son, even though we can find forgiveness when we blow it, God can't bless us until we learn our lesson and return.

Does that mean we can't spend money on ourselves or veg out in front of a mindless movie? Of course not. Being a good steward includes the occasional treats and personal expenses like taking time for relaxation or buying those new shoes you've wanted when you achieve a personal goal. God expects us to use the assets He's granted in the best way we know how. But He's waiting for us to learn that when we invest in His kingdom first, tithe, and put His blessings back into circulation, we become part of His plan to help others with those blessings.
What if you wanted to save up $10,000?

Spending vs. Saving

According to a survey by Nickelodeon and
MTV, teens are doing much better at saving
their money than most people thought.* The
13- to 21-year-olds put an average of 25
percent of their total income into savings.

So, how much are teens saving each year?
Here's what the survey said:

Age Group	Amount Saved per Year	Percent of Income Saved
13-15	$260	16%
16-17	$1,196	28%
18-21	$2,600	33%

*"U.S. Online Youth Spend $164 Billion Annually," *Business Wire*, May 15, 2001.
(www.businesswire.com/webbox/bw.091100/202553087.htm)

Three Goals of Making Money

How would you go about it? The first thing you'd need to do would be to *set your goal*.

That's easy, you might say. *The goal is to save $10,000.*

Maybe 10 Gs is the main goal, but in a case like this where it's obviously going to take a bit of doing, the goal needs to be broken down into three smaller goals.

1 The *Reason* Goal

It might help to have a reason for why you're saving. This will provide greater motivation to save when times get tough. Remember, those advertisers out there are trying to convince you they need your money. If you have a great reason behind why you're saving, it makes it less tempting to spend it.

Before you decide your reason goal, take some time to pray about it. God knows your future and He has His plans on how to get you there. The decisions you make today will affect that. Maybe He wants you to save for a car. Or college. Ask Him to direct your decision in this and help you to trust Him.

The *Time* Goal

2

Now that you've got your reason, how long will it take you to reach your goal? If saving $10,000 is your goal, $42 a week will take about four years.

The key is patience. Storing up that much happens at a snail's pace and doesn't get any faster after a few months when you start to forget why you ever thought saving this much money was a good idea. Having a specific timeframe in which to obtain your goal can help you shape your spending habits and make the saving process much easier. For example, if you're saving $10,000 for college and you start when you're 15, you'll have to develop a fairly strict spending plan. On the other hand, if you're 13, you're going to have more time.

The *Monthly* Goal

3

Figure out what your monthly goal will be by taking a look at your normal monthly finances and figuring out where the monthly income is going to come from.

How much money do you see in a normal month from an allowance, part-time job, chores around the house, and gifts? Now figure your monthly expenses: things like lunches, entertainment, shopping, tithing, gifts, and school functions. Total up everything. If you have a car, include gas, maintenance, and insurance. Subtract the expenses from your income and that's what you have left to put in savings. Most likely, if you've included all your income and outgo correctly, you don't have much of anything leftover to save. To reach your goal within the timeframe, you'll have to adjust your spending habits or figure out a way to bring in some extra cash—or both.

No one said it's easy. This is where the goal starts to seem a long way off. But with discipline and prayer, you can accomplish amazing things. "The prayer of a righteous man is powerful and effective" (James 5:16).

Five Easy Steps to Extra Cash

1. Collect change in a reliable piggy bank. Don't "raid" the piggy bank unless your intent is to put that cash into an account to begin drawing interest.

2. When your family or friends give you gifts of cash for a birthday or holiday, put it in the bank and let it earn interest.

3. It might sound silly, but coupons can really add up when you're treating yourself to a night out with friends. Some towns have "entertainment books" and student discounts at movies and restaurants. When you just can't stand another night at home with the little brother, use a coupon and put the difference of what you'd normally spend in your savings account.

4. If a parent gives you money for a new item of clothing, ask if you can put the difference in your savings account if you find a bargain. Go to an outlet, a discount store, a secondhand or consignment store, and find something similar to the brand you wanted. This tactic can be tricky though so ask your parents first and don't just buy something you won't wear in order to save some money. If you only like the price of an outfit, when it comes to actually *wearing* it you could end up wasting money.

5. Take old items—trinkets, toys, CDs, games, clothes, gear—and sell them. Some people make a pretty good second income through Internet consignment and auction sites. You can also take your stuff to pawn shops or regular consignment stores for either store credit or cash. You'd be surprised how much you can save when you simply trade in your old clothes for new stuff at consignment stores.

Spending Wisely

Bottom line: You can only save money if you get money and don't spend it. When you see a store advertising a sale that includes the words "Buy now and save!" keep in mind that you'll probably still end up spending just as much before you get the savings. Chances are you'll end up with more than you need. Twelve scrunchies for the price of eight isn't a deal. Who needs a dozen scrunchies, let alone eight?

To keep from spending more than you have to, try the following:

- **Defend against impulse buys.** Rule of thumb: If it seems like a deal you just can't pass up, it's probably a deal you *should* pass up.

- **Always ask yourself "the questions" before you make a purchase.** "Do I really need this?" "Can I live without this item?" "Will the benefit outweigh the cost?"

- **Carry only the cash you need when you're going out—and never carry credit cards to a sale.** If you're prone to the temptation to spend, remove the danger.

- **When you shop, don't linger.** Make a list of the purchases you've decided to make and stick to it. Don't give yourself a chance to be tempted to spend more than you should.

- **Never buy what you can get for free.** Don't purchase *anything*—CDs, video games, DVDs, videos, books, tapes, magazines, software—if you can borrow from a friend, or the library, or get it free online. Copyrights prevent you from copying these things, but for example, renting a movie you might watch a few times is much cheaper than buying it. And often, a good library will have it for free. Remember, it will always be true that what's hot today will be lame tomorrow. Smart stewards don't waste their money.

The Part-Time Job: How to Get One

"Kim! What're you doin' Friday night?" My best friend, Jamie, was glowing.

"Nothing, yet."

"Okay, here's the plan. We're going downtown to MacKenzie's Grill, catch the 7:30 movie, and then heading to Starbucks to hear Crusted Jam play. *Then* on Saturday we're going to the new mall to shop all day!" She was pretty excited. Her voice was coming out in one long, rambling word.

"Sounds like fun," I said reluctantly. "But I can't come. I'm saving money."

Jamie looked at me, suddenly apologetic. "Well . . . at least come check out the mall with us tomorrow."

I shrugged and tried to sound excited. "Alright. Thanks."

Can you relate to Kim? Never have any money to hang out with friends? Maybe they all have part-time jobs (or maybe Mommy and Daddy help out) to pay for their fun, but that doesn't mean you should have to miss out entirely. There are plenty of good jobs out there just waiting to get you some expendable income!

Some teens work a few hours a week and have a blast on the weekends. Others have after-school activities, work various hours on the weekends, and fit their fun in between. If you feel left out of enjoying the full social life that your friends have, or your parents are getting on your case about college and you need to start saving, here are a few tips to help you land the perfect job.

1. **Assess your situation.** Take a look at your class load. No matter how broke you are, classes always come first. You're a high school student first and a worker second.

2. **Plan your workload.** Time to ask some questions. What's your goal? Realistically, how much do you want to earn? How many hours per week will you need to work? At what hourly rate? Factor in how much you need to save (for things like college or car maintenance) and how much you can spend beyond the basics (like car insurance, gas, phone bill, etc.). Take the time to plan right now so you won't be surprised how rapidly your paycheck gets eaten up.

3. **Brainstorm.** This is the fun part. What are your interests; what do you like doing? Keep in mind that you're not looking for a career, you just need money. And preferably, it will involve something you enjoy, but for now, nothing is too "out there" to consider: Maybe you just love the county fair and there's a hot dog stand that needs a vendor. Whatever you enjoy, there's a perfect part-time job to match it.

4. **Locate the possibilities.** Make a list of your ideas that fit your interests and start looking for businesses that involve those things and employ part-time help. What specific places could you apply to? If "I love kids" was on your list of interests, find the day care centers in your phone book. Talk to people at your church about their work. Do you have an "in" anywhere? Maybe your dad owns a business or your neighborhood has a community swimming pool you could lifeguard for.

5. **Get out there.** Put on your favorite outfit, grab the car keys (or recruit Mom or Dad for a ride), and start visiting the places you thought of. Visiting in person rather than sending a resume (next chapter) over the fax or even calling on the phone is a much better way to land the job you want. When you walk inside, remember to smile! There's no reason to be nervous. Simply ask to speak with the manager (it's better to meet face-to-face with the person who has hiring power), introduce yourself, and ask for an application. Ask if they're hiring and for which positions. Once you've gotten the application, thank the manager for his/her time and head to the next place.

6. **Go back.** After you've collected all the applications and weeded out the places that won't work, fill out the applications, get any recommendations you need, and return them. Ask for the manager again and warmly greet him or her. Want bonus points? Remember his or her name! Tell him you are very interested in the position and you'll be looking forward to his call.

7. **Wait patiently, but persistently.** Now the ball is in the manager's court to call. Wait a week or so and if you haven't heard back, make a call to ask about the status of your application. This provides another opportunity to say you're interested and excited about the job.

9. **Follow through.** If you get called for an interview, come prepared with what you hope to gain from the job. Any questions you can think of (such as whether or not they pay for your training) should be asked now. Based on the information you gather, you'll be able to tell if the job is right for you or not. Above all, *relax and be yourself.* Employers want employees who are able to roll with the punches and take things in stride. The interview is an opportunity for both you and the employer to find out if you're a good candidate for the position. If you are, it will become obvious when you're relaxed and being yourself.

The Resume

So, you want that part-time job, but they require a resume. How do you go about it?

Basically, a resume is just a list of your experiences. Some employers like to see on paper what you've accomplished and what your goals are. Sometimes it's hard for employers to see the human being beyond the piece of paper, so it's good advice to make your resume as personal as you can. Show the employer that you are much more than your list of experiences will ever be! And what you lack in experience right now, you make up for in personality and passion for your goals.

Resume writing isn't as daunting as it may seem. Basically, it's like an advertisement to sell a product to a specific target market—except *you* are the product and the target is the company you'll eventually work for. Think about what you want to show on your resume. What would convince you to hire you? Get personal. What hobbies do you enjoy? How do you spend your free time? What subjects in school interest you? Are you involved in any clubs or sports or other activities? Outside your likes and dislikes, keep thinking specifically about *you*. What in your personality makes you unique? Do you thrive around people and activity? Or are you good at paying attention to details? Highlighting these things shows you know yourself!

Now start writing down your "relative experience." In this section, list any jobs or volunteer positions you've had. Did you pick blueberries on a farm last summer? Do you occasionally baby-sit your little sister? Have you house-sat for neighbors or taken part in a play? Think big—even if it wasn't about getting paid, you've done some cool things worth mentioning.

Write every thought down as it comes to you and don't edit yet. The point of this process is to get to know yourself and see what you have to offer.

Next you'll need to answer some technical questions. If you have a computer, you may be able to use one of the formats that come ready-made. How can you format the information in a way that shows your best features? How can you bring it all together? Pay a visit to a library, or a bookstore, or cruise some Web sites on resume building. There is a ton of materials on putting together a compelling resume.

Resume building also helps you think about your experiences and your strengths as you prepare for the interview. Being familiar with the paper version of you ensures you'll know what to say with honesty and confidence.

Part Seven
Tough Stuff

Q: What's so bad about alcohol and drugs?

A: There are a lot of conflicting attitudes about alcohol use, even among Christians. For example, your friend's parents may believe it's okay to drink alcohol within limits, while your own parents may believe drinking is strictly off-limits for Christians. While this is a question that each family needs to carefully consider, the fact remains that alcohol and drugs can have deadly consequences.

While some teens say drugs and alcohol are just harmless fun, the truth is 120,000 deaths are caused every year by alcohol and drugs, and most sexual assaults among teenagers are preceded by drinking. You may know teens who use yet do well in school; they start on the football or basketball team. They seem to have no problems holding it together. They're definitely not the losers some adults would have you believe. It sure looks like they're having a lot of fun. It's hard not to catch yourself wondering what all the hype is about.

But beyond all the excuses, the exaggerated dangers, and hype, the truth is that no alcoholic or drug addict started out thinking they'd become addicted. The real consequences associated with these chemicals are how they change you.

Just as the body has a delicate balance to maintain in keeping strong and healthy, you must also constantly guard your spirit against anything that would disrupt the balance and pull it away from its life-giving source: God. When foreign substances come in and set up shop in your body, pain and suffering are the natural result.

In our self-centered society, rampant drug and alcohol use is a reality. Yet equally real is the fact that our bodies, minds, and spirits weren't meant to deal with the toxins of mind-altering drugs. That's the reason they're called "mind-altering"—they disrupt the normal functioning and cause alterations in the body's natural balance. Whenever that balance is thrown off, pain is the inevitable result. There is a long list of complications caused by substances with which the body doesn't work well: hangovers, chronic headaches, cancers, dehydration, brain damage, impaired motor response, etc. Unfortunately, many people begin using alcohol or drugs to escape one kind of pain and end up with an entirely different kind.

The bottom line is that if you're choosing to substitute a chemical for God, sooner or later you will come to unhappiness, brokenness, and pain. But if none of that can convince you not to fool around with drugs and alcohol, let it be the fact that God owns your body and doesn't want to see you give it to anything unworthy.

*Adapted from the booklet "Lethal Haze: The Vicious Truth About Drugs & Alcohol," Dare 2 Dig Deeper series, ©1998 Focus on the Family.

Q: How do I know if I have an eating disorder?

A: Ask yourself the following questions

- Do you get nervous thinking about social situations where you'll have to eat?

- Do you have strict rituals for eating (do you follow a determined order, try to prevent foods from touching, stick to a limited menu, cut food into tiny pieces, or compulsively trim fat)?

- Do you feel good or bad depending on how much you eat, weigh, or exercise?

- Does weighing too much make you keep to yourself? As a result, when you feel lonely, does your strictness about your diet increase?

- Do you spend a lot of time thinking about food (how much you eat or will eat)?

- Have you used laxatives, vomiting, pills, or excessive exercise to help you lose weight or to gain control over your weight?

- Would you eat more if you didn't control yourself?

- Do you sometimes feel out of control when eating and frequently eat beyond the point of fullness to the point of physical discomfort?

- Are you frequently depressed because you feel fat or overweight?

- Do you diet or fast (other than for spiritual purposes) weekly or monthly?

- Do you feel if you could lose weight that you could achieve all your other goals?

- Do you restrict your eating or overeat when you are stressed or feel unhappy?

Although these questions do not necessarily indicate that you have an eating disorder, if you answered "yes" to many of them you should get help. Many girls (even from Christian homes) think they can play around with an eating disorder for a while and stop before it gets out of control. But an eating disorder isn't something you can play around with. You know the statement "You are what you eat"? Well, it works the other way too. The less you eat, the less able you are to think logically and make good decisions. Before you make food your enemy, talk to someone you trust. Parents, youth pastors, and school counselors can help. You may find out that someone you know went through the same thing when she was your age and can help you gain perspective on your situation.

Note: If you do choose to participate in activities that put you at risk for eating disorders (including gymnastics, dance, ballet, swimming, or modeling), make yourself accountable to a couple of mature, objective people, such as a school nurse, counselor, youth pastor, or prayer partner. Parents, coaches, and friends can sometimes be too close to the situation to be objective accountability partners.

And remember: The same God the psalmist wrote about in Psalm 139 who knew him intimately is the One who holds intimate knowledge about your future plans for your life. When you feel yourself being tempted to measure yourself against the world's arbitrary standards, take time to meditate on the truth that God knows everything about you—and loves you just the way you are. "O LORD, you have searched me and you know me." Psalm 139:1.

If you think you are struggling with an eating disorder, please call 1-800-A-FAMILY and ask to speak to a counselor. They can recommend some local counselors, books, and other materials that will help.

When you call, ask for the booklet "Beyond Appearances: The Truth About Eating Disorders" (in the Dare 2 Dig Deeper series from which this information was adapted), Eating Disorders by Phyllis Alsdurf and James Alsdurf [InterVarsity], and Escaping Anorexia and Bulimia by Donald Durham and Dr. Paul Hanson (booklet).

Q: A close friend of mine just died. I'm having a hard time.

A: When someone you know dies, it's important to accept your feelings and face your sadness so you can start getting on with your own life. By learning to deal with grief and loss, you can save yourself unnecessary heartache down the road. It can get better, and your biggest chance to come out of your grief is to understand your emotions and work through them with courage. Most importantly, be sure you talk to a trained counselor or a psychologist you trust to get help in processing your natural feelings.

Here are some of the basic tasks a psychologist or grief counselor can help you to address:

1. **Accept the reality of the loss.** Shock and denial are normal, understandable responses to loss. Yet you can help yourself tremendously by doing all you can to accept that the death has occurred and needs to be confronted.

2. **Work through the pain.** Once you realize you aren't going to wake up from this dream, you begin to understand that your life has changed. You may realize feelings of anger, resentment, or betrayal you are holding against the deceased. It's important not to feel guilty, but to deal with your feelings as honestly as possible. Often, the process will progress in five steps: identifying what specific attachments you've lost, feeling the pain, telling your story to others, dealing with regrets and resentments (e.g. survivor's guilt), and finally, taking time to look forward. Again, a qualified professional is in the best position to help you deal with these issues one step at a time.

3. **Accept your world with the loss.** Despair can be a powerful trap for those without a higher hope. If you feel that you can't go on in this world without this person, remember that plenty of people have climbed out of that same pit of despair and you eventually will too. Your emotions are working exactly as God designed them to work to ultimately push you forward. Give yourself time to feel everything your heart is experiencing and don't worry! When you're ready to move on, you will.

4. **Have a place for memories, but move on.** Soon, you'll realize there are some specific things you can do to claim life in this new world. The old axiom, Every ending is a new beginning, is true. Memories and sadness remain, but you'll have a real strength now to move on. You'll feel small stirrings of hope and purpose again. During this stage, reaching out to others who may be hurting can help you focus on something meaningful. Realize that God wants to use you as an example to others.

No two people grieve the same. No one should expect you to be expressing or acting on something you aren't ready for. Neither should you be expecting someone else to be at the same place in the process as you are. For teen girls, it's especially important to be on guard that you don't accept an unhealthy situation in your need for comfort. When your heart is suffering from a deep wound, it's no time to be putting yourself in a situation where a desire for affection or intimacy could get out of control. Think ahead before accepting social engagements that could require you to stretch your personal boundaries when you're in this weakened state. Your real friends will understand and respect your decision. By the same token, don't unnecessarily isolate yourself when trying to work through grief. Continue as many of your normal activities as you can, realizing that you may need to forego some for the time being.

*Adapted from the booklet "Good Grief: A Healthy, Courageous Response to Loss," Dare 2 Dig Deeper series, ©2000 Focus on the Family.

Q: What is sexual harassment? I've been in situations where a guy makes me feel weird but should I do something about it?

A: Federal regulations define sexual harassment as: "unwelcome sexual advances, requests for sexual favors, and other verbal and physical conduct of a sexual nature." When someone uses sexual harassment . . .

- as a condition for employment, performance evaluation, class attendance, or academic progress,

- as a basis for a decision he/she has to make,

- or for the purpose of intimidating, offending, or interfering with your life,

you have certain legal rights in dealing with the offender.

Victims of sexual harassment do not share any dominant characteristics other than the fact that over 99 percent are female. Studies have shown that the effects can be devastating. Women of all ages have reported experiencing feelings from anxiety to insecurity, embarrassment, confusion, fear, and powerlessness. Many women feel so helpless that they eventually change their jobs, majors—even their lifestyles.

Silence is not a solution! By ignoring or denying the situation, you are allowing this behavior to continue. Your harasser may even interpret your silence as permission. Instead:

1. **Place the blame where it belongs—on the harasser!** Don't blame yourself, which just leads to further problems.

2. **Clearly state your disapproval.** Say "no" or "stop," and be direct. Express yourself immediately, or it may occur again. Sometimes it's a gentle response, such as, "Please don't compliment me in that way; it makes me feel uncomfortable," other times something more firm is warranted:

"That's sexual harassment. Someone in authority will hear about this."

3. **Tell someone in authority.** A teacher, your school counselor, a parent, a boss.

4. **After you've given your warning, keep a record of any recurrence.** Record the time, place, action, and words so that if you are asked to present your case, you can do so.

5. **Be persistent.** Whoever you've told about this, make sure they are handling the issue, and don't give up. Sometimes it takes time to get your case heard.

*Adapted from the booklet "A Crime of Force," Dare 2 Dig Deeper series, ©1998 Focus on the Family.

Q: I've heard a lot about date rape and I'm worried. How can I know if a guy is safe to be with?

Here are some warning signs of an unsafe guy.

A:
• **He is ultra-confident, charming, and engaging.** A guy's charm can be a dangerous tool. Don't buy into it.

• **He displays anger, crude humor, and negativity toward women.** Unsafe guys get hostile when they don't get their way. They might tell crude or misogynistic (women-hating) jokes. He might say a girl is a "tease" or call her "uptight."

• **He persists in trying to get women alone.** The best way to be safe with an unsafe guy is to never be alone with him. Always staying in a group lets you get to know a guy *before* being alone.

• **He ignores women's personal space and likes to touch.** Unsafe guys test the boundaries to see how far they can get. Sometimes a girl won't react, not wanting to be rude, and the guy will interpret this as approval. Protect yourself by always asserting your concerns and remembering that no one has a right to your body. If a guy can't respect the boundaries, he shouldn't be allowed to hang around.

Adapted from the article "Five Warning Signs of a Potential Date Rapist" by Me Ra Koh, *Brio & Beyond,* Dec. 2001. For more warning signs like these, ask for the article, or the booklet "Avoiding Rape On and Off Campus" by Carol Pritchard. The book *Beauty Restored: Finding Life and Hope After Date Rape* by Me Ra Koh is available from Focus on the Family (1-800-A-FAMILY).

Q: I think my friend's dad may be abusive, but I'm not sure. Is there something I can do?

A: Yes. You should report any case of abuse to the police to help save a friend. Reports indicate that one out of every four girls (and one out of eight boys) will be sexually abused before they turn 18. The number of reported cases every year is in the millions. Even with the increase in reporting, studies estimate that only one in 20 cases is ever reported. Eighty percent of the cases involve adults the victim knows, loves, or trusts (according to *Steering Them Straight,* by Stephen Arterburn and Jim Burns [Focus on the Family]).

Of course, it's important to get all the facts you can before you make a judgment. If you accuse a friend's parent of abuse and it turns out you're wrong, you could cause a lot of trouble for your friend's family. Before you go damaging anyone's reputation, make sure you have good reason to believe there is actual verbal or physical abuse taking place. The definition of *abuse* is any verbal or physical action intended to damage the individual. Sometimes abuse can be difficult to determine, but if seeing some of the clues is causing you to wonder, chances are there's something not right about the situation.

Some girls experience verbal abuse from a family member, others get the brunt of physical abuse from a father or brother. You may have a friend who's been the victim of sexual abuse in her home. If you're experiencing any kind of abuse, we encourage you to break the silence and ask a trusted adult for help. This might be a youth leader, your pastor, a school counselor, or a favorite teacher. (You should be aware that a licensed counselor is required to report abuse to the authorities.)

Because families are made up of humans, and because no human is perfect, all families will struggle. It could be that your friend is living with an *irregular family.* Maybe she isn't being abused, but things just don't seem right much of the time.

Perhaps her dad is extremely prejudiced. Or her mom limits the number of Sundays she can attend church. This isn't abuse, but neither is it normal—it's *irregular.*

Even if you aren't sure whether or not your friend is living with an irregular parent, it's important that you encourage her to find a healthy role model. If one of your parents isn't a good choice, is there an adult in your church she could open up with and trust? Ask God to help you find an adult whom you could approach about mentoring your friend.

In the same way, if you're in a situation like this, you need to find an adult you can trust as well. When you've found one, ask her if the two of you can get together twice a month. Explain to her that you love and respect your parents but that there are times you need someone else's input. Pray that this godly woman will be a huge spiritual influence on you. Strive to develop a healthy relationship with her that will allow the two of you to talk about anything, pray, and sort through tough issues together.

We don't get to choose our families. But God has placed these people in our lives for a reason. Ask Him to help you see through His eyes—not your own. And determine that you'll learn important lessons from dealing with them—lessons such as patience, honesty, and discernment.

If you or a friend has been abused, please call Focus on the Family and ask for the counseling department (1-800-A-FAMILY). Our counselors can help you sort through your pain and will refer you to a licensed counselor near you as well.

Adapted from the booklet "When Someone You Know Is Sexually Abused" from the Let's Talk About Life series by Susie Shellenberger, available from Focus on the Family.

Q: What is incest?

A: Incest is sexual activity among family members, the most common type of sexual abuse. Incest may be covert (concealed or less obvious) or overt (out in the open and blatant). Whether it's covert or overt, it's still sexual abuse and it's always a crime. Incest has been reported in every country in every era.

Incest most frequently happens to children and young adults. If you've experienced incest, you may have a hard time knowing what kind of affection is normal in families. Hugging and kissing, patting each other on the back, and even playful wrestling or tickling are normal. But if a family member touches you in a private area, or does any of these things forcefully, that is NOT normal and is considered incestuous.

If a friend is trapped in an abusive situation, you might notice:

- Low self-esteem

- Difficulty having good relationships with the opposite sex

- Self-mutilation (cutting or burning herself)

- Reacting defensively when touched

- Dramatic changes in attitude or performance

- Complaints of frequent pains

- Withdrawn or depressed attitude

- Unusual eating issues (eats too much or too little)

- Extreme hostility toward parents or authority figures

- Overreacting or quick temper

- Fear of darkness, basements, closets

- Feelings of unworthiness

Though some of these characteristics can result from other problems, if you notice a friend displaying several of these, it may be a sign of sexual abuse. Share your suspicions with a trusted adult, but don't go spreading rumors and misinformation. The reputation of your friend's family is on the line. Get the facts first, then gently approach your friend and let her know you can be trusted. Remind her how much you care about her and value her friendship. She may not share her problem right away, but the important thing is that you stand by her—especially when you see she's struggling.

If you or a friend is dealing with incest, it's important to know that sexual violation may be reality, but no one needs to live in fear. No matter how bad the nightmare is, it's not hopeless. Help is always available.

If you have been a victim of incest, please call Focus on the Family and ask for the counseling department (1-800-A-FAMILY). Our counselors can help you sort through your pain and will refer you to a licensed counselor near you as well.

Adapted from the booklet
"When Someone You Know Is Sexually Abused"
from the Let's Talk About Life series by Susie Shellenberger,
available from Focus on the Family.

Q: There is so much conflicting information about abortion. What's the truth?

A: Pregnancy is an amazing growth process. Psalm 139 says that God created it and has a plan for each baby's life. The instant an egg and sperm unite, the embryo develops the DNA plans for every stage of its development, including gender, hair and eye color, and height. At three weeks after conception the baby has a heartbeat. Brain waves are detected at six weeks. Nine weeks, and the baby's body has internal organs, fingerprints, and responds to touch. The mother may not feel movement until four or five months, but the fetus is much more than "a blob of tissue."

Abortion providers typically don't give women the facts on fetal development. For example, when Stacy went to an abortion clinic, she says, "No one gave me any information about what was going to happen. They said things like, 'You're going to feel a little bit of pressure here,' but as far as the actual abortion procedure, I was never told." Another young woman, Kiersa, says, "It was painful . . . It went on, it seemed like, forever."

Today there are many options for ending a pregnancy. But every option kills a baby before it's had a chance to be born. Some procedures cut the baby's body into pieces. With these techniques, there are risks of hemorrhage, infection, and damage to the reproductive system. At four months of development, saline may be injected into the uterus with a long needle. The mother goes into labor and delivers a dead baby. And late in pregnancy, there's dilation and extraction (D&X), also known as partial-birth abortion. Also, any type of abortion increases the risk of breast cancer because it alters pregnancy's natural breast development.

As far as emotional effects go, Stacy recalls, "After the procedure was over, I was taken into another room. I remember crying uncontrollably and not really understanding why. I became detached and unemotional. I didn't want anything to ever hurt me like that again. . . . I didn't want to have anything to do with my boyfriend. I felt like I was unprotected—that he really didn't care about me."

Many women struggle with sadness, anger, guilt, and flashbacks as a result of abortion—even years after. The good news is that God cares about every person affected by abortion. Psalm 34:18 says, "The LORD is close to the brokenhearted," and Psalm 30:11 says God can turn mourning into dancing. Many girls have discovered this, but it's a long climb out of the pit of pain. Don't let fear and misinformation lead you or a friend into the abortion trap.

If you (or a friend) need comfort or advice in dealing with abortion, call Focus on the Family's Crisis Pregnancy Ministry at 719-531-3460 (or 1-800-A-FAMILY). The staff can give you information about a Pregnancy Resource Center near you.

*Adapted from the article "The Truth About Abortion" by Lindy Beam, *Brio*, Jan. 2003.

Conclusion

We've talked about a lot, haven't we? Everything from temptation to TV to tithing!

Hopefully, what you've read has sparked some questions. And you know who we'd like to steer you toward? You know who has the best advice? Jesus Christ. Since He's the One who created you, He knows you better than you even know yourself!

How about letting us pray with you? All you have to do is read along.

Dear Jesus:

This growing up stuff is going to be tough. There are so many changes I'll probably get confused a lot. I'd sure like it if You could help me.

Jesus, I don't want to try to run my own life. Will You take charge of me? I give You total control right now. I know You are able to make me a brand new person in Your image. I believe the Bible is Your Holy Word—absolute truth. And I believe You died for my sins. I don't deserve it Jesus, but I'm grateful. Help me to live a life that's pleasing to You. Give me a hunger and thirst for Your Word. Help me to find a strong group of friends at church and a good Bible study to get involved in. I realize this is just the beginning of a huge relationship with You.

I trust You, Jesus. I don't know what my future holds, but I know that You're holding everything that's in it. I love You so much.

Amen.

Hey, we really do want to hear from you! Drop us a line sometime, okay?

briomag@macmail.fotf.org

—Susie Shellenberger

The Food Pyramid
A Guide to Daily Food Choices

U.S. Department of Agriculture/U.S. Department of Health and Human Services

Fats, Oils, and Sweets
Use sparingly

Meats, Poultry, Fish, Beans,
Eggs, and Nuts Group
2-3 Servings

Milk, Yogurt, and
Cheese Group
2-3 Servings

Vegetable Group
3-5 Servings

Fruit Group
2-4 Servings

Bread, Cereal, Rice and Pasta Group
6-11 Servings

Grow

At Focus on the Family, we are committed to helping you learn more about Jesus Christ and preparing you to change your world for Him! We realize the struggles you face are different from your parent's or your little brother's, so Focus on the Family has developed a ton of stuff specifically for you! They'll get you ready to boldly live out your faith no matter what situation you find yourself in.

We don't want to tell you what to do. We want to encourage and equip you to be all God has called you to be in every aspect of life! That may involve strengthening your relationship with God, solidifying your values and perhaps making some serious changes in your heart and mind.

We'd like to come alongside you as you consider God's role in your life, discover His plan for you in the lives of others and how you can impact your generation to change the world.

We have Web sites, magazines, palm-sized topical booklets, fiction books, a live call-in radio show ... all dealing with the topics and issues that you deal with and care about. For a more detailed listing of what we have available to you, visit our Web site at **www.family.org** and click on 'resources,' followed by either 'teen girls' or 'teen guys.'